A Love Like That

Exulon
ELITE

A Love Like That

GOD'S WHOLEHEARTED AND HEALING AFFECTION FOR HIS DAUGHTERS

Margie Fleurant

A Love Like That
God's Wholehearted and Healing Affection for His Daughters
Copyright © 2014—Margie Fleurant

The River Ministries
P.O. Box 287
Martinsville, NJ 08836
margiefleurant.org

ISBN: 9781498416238

Book cover and interior layout: www.swinghousedesign.com
Printed in the United States of America.

Dedication

I dedicate this book to my precious daughters, Danielle and Jaclyn.

Acknowledgments

Thank You to Holy Spirit, who inspired this entire book.

Thank you to my family. They have been a constant source of love and support—especially my husband, John. Because of your unwavering, continual support, I have been able to do all God has put in my heart. Together we make a great team, and one day we will stand before God and see all the lives that have been changed through our ministry.

A special thanks to my closest confidants, who have supported me, inspired me, and poured into me their love, faithfulness, and friendship.

Thank you to Amy Calkins, my gift from God.

Contents

Introduction

This book was inspired by a 2011 women's conference entitled "The Consuming Fire of God's Love." Over the course of just two days, many women encountered the love of God in a way that truly transformed their lives and rewrote their personal stories.

God wants to do the same for you through this book.

Each one of us has a story. Our lives are like history books—with accounts of victory as well as pain, happy times and tearful times. But no matter what the theme of our history has been or where we are in the progression of our story, when we encounter the love of God, we are changed. That old chapter ends, and a new chapter begins. God does not hold onto the past but promises to do a new thing in us (see Isa. 43:19; 65:17). As you encounter God's love through the pages of this book, I declare freshness, newness, wisdom, and increased revelation over you. God wants to do a new thing for you.

When life's story begins to be painful or boring or full of distractions, it is easy to forget why we're here and what this is all about. It is easy to forget we are dearly loved daughters of a King, to forget we have swords in our hands because we are overcomers. But it's true. When we face the difficulties of life, we are not like a swordless army. We are not defenseless against the enemy's schemes. Encountering the love of God reminds us of that—and it sharpens our swords to do battle more brilliantly.

God has incredible plans for His daughters. He made women for a powerful purpose, and He put swords in our hands. God, the most intelligent being in existence, made and chose us for something great—and He doesn't make mistakes. When life runs us over, He reminds us, "I love you!" He puts that sword back in our hands. And He turns the page to a new chapter.

I believe this book can be the beginning of something new for you. God wants to declare His love to you in these pages and take you deeper into relationship with Him. If you let Him, I know you will never be the same again.

At the conference, God gave me this prophecy for the women there, and I want to declare it over you as well:

This is the dawn of a new day, and I the Lord have prepared the way. I've gone before you, and I've prepared the way. I'm going to make some really hard times for you straight. Some crooked thinking plain. My glory is going to be revealed, and I'm going to send abundance of rain. I'm going to send refreshing from My presence, and it's going to wash away all the stains. It's going to wash away all the guilt, and it's going to wash away the weights and the sins that have so easily beset you. Because what I promised unto you, My daughters, I am going to make good. So know that I have ordained this time.

Know that you are in this place right on time, and I am going to do exceedingly, abundantly above all you have already asked, hoped, dreamed, or desired.

One of the amazing things about God's love is that it literally transforms us. We cannot encounter His love and stay the same. That's what this book is all about—encountering and understanding the love of God and then knowing how to daily walk in relationship with Him and growing revelation of the fire of His love for you. Through this process, you will step into greater rest, strength, and ability to overcome sin. His perfect love will cast out fears that have bound you and free you from toxic habits and relationships. Truly, as you turn these pages, I believe you are turning the pages of your life, stepping into a new chapter about a new woman who has been strengthened and beautified in the love of God.

Welcome to the beginning of your new story.

PART 1

Consumed by His Love

We humans were made for love. From birth, we crave it and will sacrifice almost anything to find it. Without it, we cannot be emotionally or physically healthy. Even babies, who have no mental concept of love, can die simply from a lack of physical touch and loving interaction. We can literally shrivel up and die from love starvation. Our need for love is at our core. It is who we are.

It is no wonder our culture thrives on love songs and love stories, on fairytales and prince charming. This is what we were made for from the very beginning. When God created Adam and Eve in the Garden of Eden, He created them as recipients of His magnificent and unending love. He designed them as vessels to constantly be filled and overflowing with the vibrancy of His delight in them. When they walked away from His love, they found themselves incomplete. They suddenly realized they were empty vessels with a love vacuum—and they had rejected the only one with the capacity to fill it.

This problem of epic proportions has been passed down to every human since, and it has defined the course of human history. More than any other descriptor—more than wealth, class, education, family name, race, nationality, time period, religion—our experience of love defines us. It is the litmus test that determines who we will be and how we will live on this earth.

Fortunately, although humanity foolishly walked away from God, He made a way to reconcile us back to Himself because of His love for us. He made the greatest sacrifice of all to bring us back into His embrace and help us find ourselves in Him. He is the answer for the love vacuum, and His love is deeper and better than we will ever know. Through the ages of separation from God's heart, humanity has struggled to understand what love really is. In the process, people have cheapened and distorted it, because they did not know the one who is love. That is what Part 1 of this book is about—encountering His love and finding ourselves in Him.

CHAPTER 1

The Fruit of Love

The Bible often depicts people as trees who bear fruit. In Psalm 1 the righteous person is compared to *"a tree planted by streams of water, which yields its fruit in season and whose leaf does not whither"* (Ps. 1:3). And Jesus famously said, *"Make a tree good and its fruit will be good, or make a tree bad and its fruit will be bad, for a tree is recognized by its fruit"* (Matt. 12:33). In other words, like trees, we bear outward fruit that reveals the condition of our inward lives.

Also, like trees, our internal health is determined by the water we drink and the soil we spread our roots in. Trees that produce good fruit have an abundant and unpolluted water supply and room to spread out their roots in oxygen-rich soil. The depth of a tree's roots is directly connected to the amount of oxygen in the layers of soil beneath it. Similarly, people who bear good fruit are rooted and established in the good soil of God's love. The soil of our lives is what determines the quality of our inner lives and, therefore, our outward fruit. This is exactly what Paul referred to when he wrote about the importance of being strengthened in the inner person:

> *I pray that out of his glorious riches he may* **strengthen you with power through his Spirit in your inner being,** *so that Christ may dwell in your hearts through faith. And I pray that you,* **being rooted and established in love,** *may have power, together with all the Lord's holy people, to grasp how wide and long and high and deep is the love of Christ, and to know this love that surpasses knowledge—that you may be* **filled to the measure of all the fullness of God** (Ephesians 3:16–19).

Here we see three progressive steps for how to bear good fruit. First, we are strengthened internally when we invite Christ to dwell in our hearts through faith. Second, we are rooted and established in His love and begin to comprehend the great extent of God's love for us. Third, as a result of encountering God's love, we are filled to the measure of the fullness of God.

God wants us to comprehend how wide, long, high, and deep the fire of His love is for each one of us. This is not a shallow or easily offended affection. This is, in the truest sense, true love. Children's stories and fairy tales talk about the power of true love's kiss, but we have the truest love's kiss in the extravagant and fiery love of God. In the recent animated movie, *Frozen*, the sisters, Ana and Elsa, learn that only an act of true love can thaw a frozen heart. And as it turns out, the necessary act of love is not the kiss of a prince but the sacrifice of a sister. This is an imperfect picture of the true love–inspired sacrifice in which Christ gave His own life to thaw our frozen hearts. To turn us from people who bear bad fruit into those who bear good fruit.

When we encounter and begin to understand love like this, love that surpasses all knowledge, we are drastically changed. As Jesus told His disciples, *"I am the vine; you are the branches. If you remain in me and I in you, you will **bear** much **fruit**; apart from me you can do nothing"* (John 15:5). Without an ever increasing revelation of His love, we have no hope of becoming fruitful. Only in His love will we blossom and bloom into the women He has made us to be. Truly His love is no ordinary love. Solomon describes true love like this:

> *Place me like a seal over your heart, like a seal on your arm; for love is as strong as death, its jealousy unyielding as the grave. It burns like blazing fire, like a mighty flame. Many waters cannot quench love; rivers cannot sweep it away. If one were to give all the wealth of one's house for love, it would be utterly scorned* (Song of Solomon 8:6–7).

That is how intense God's love is for each one of us. In fact, while Solomon's song says love is as strong as death, Jesus has shown us that His love is actually stronger than death. Now *"neither death nor life...nor anything else in all creation will be able to separate us from the love of God that is in Christ Jesus our Lord"* (Rom. 8:38–39). His love has overcome it all.

Not only does God *have* love for us, but the Bible tells us *"God is love"* (1 John 4:8, 16). In His nature He embodies and defines love. We know what love looks like by looking at Him. The Bible also tells us, *"God is a consuming fire"* (Heb. 12:29). This is the nature of His love toward us—consuming and fiery.

Consuming is defined as "ardent, deeply felt, possessing or displaying a distinctive feature to a heightened degree, very intense, strongly and urgently felt." When something is consumed, it is devoured. This is what happens when we accept Christ and "die" with Him so we can be raised with Him into new life (see Rom. 6:3–4). God's consuming love burns out the negative in us. Now we no longer bear bad fruit. Instead, we are the righteousness of God in Christ Jesus (see 2 Cor. 5:21). We are fearfully and wonderfully made (see Ps. 139:14). He is rooting us in His love and consuming the negative thinking and harmful patterns in our lives so we can live in His fullness. Our roots are growing deeper into the oxygen-rich soil of His love, and now we bear good fruit.

> *God's love is consuming, and it is a fire.*

God's love is consuming, and it is a *fire*. It burns like a mighty flame. Uncontrolled fire is inherently consuming. It burns up whatever stands in its path. Thus, the fire of God's love burns away anything that should not exist in our lives as new creations. It burns up the lies that tell us we're not worth much, and it replaces them with the truth of His passion for us and our incalculable worth to Him. It burns up the pain and rejection and fear of our past and replaces them with hope and joy and peace—with the blessed fruit of His Spirit (see Gal. 5:22–23).

In the natural, flames of fire also produce heat. Likewise, the flame of God's love for us produces heat within us; it ignites greater passion for God in us, so we too long to be with Him. Hidden within His love is the invitation to love Him back. He has made us women with a choice. We have the power to choose Him (or not choose Him), and when we choose Him above all others, we are learning to love like He loves. We are fanned into flames by the flame in His heart, because *"God's love has been poured out into our hearts"* (Rom. 5:5).

I like to tell God, "I am deeply in love with You. You're deeply in love with me, and I'm deeply in love with You, too." When He tells me He loves me with an everlasting love (see Jer. 31:3), I reciprocate. I tell Him, "I love you with an everlasting love, too!" And I feel it and think it with all my heart, all my soul, all my mind, and all my strength (see Mark 12:30). I give my love back to Him with all I am.

About this, Saint Augustine once said, "Let us love God with the love he has given us."[1] In other words, we are only capable of loving Him with the love He first gives to us. *"We love Him because He first loved us"* (1 John 4:19 NKJV). And that is exactly what He wants us to do. He wants us to return His love with all we have. He wants us to be passionate. We don't have to be afraid of giving Him our all, because He will never reject or ignore us. He is the safest and kindest person we will ever meet, and He is our King, our Creator, our Father. He is the lover of our souls.

> *"Let us love God with the love he has given us."*

When we are touched by this flame of His love, we will want to spend time with Him—which is exactly how He feels about us. His heart burns for us constantly. His eyes are always upon us, and His desire is always for us. He will never lose interest in us. His appetite for us will never wane, and we will never be able to exhaust the depths of relationship with Him. That is the nature of His consuming, fiery love. The more we experience Him, the more we want to experience Him. And so, in a glorious and eternal cycle of increase, we will forever go deeper and deeper in love with Him, endeavoring to somehow comprehend the height, depth, breadth, and length of the love of Christ that surpasses knowledge (see Eph. 3:18).

Our revelation of the love of God never ends; it just keeps growing bigger and brighter and stronger. While His love for us is constant and the strength of His passion for us never changes, our passion for Him will increase as we encounter His love for us. As we are rooted and established in His love, we will become lovers like Him. And truly we will be transformed into trees who bear His fruit.

This is true love. And it is the only love that will truly satisfy the desires of our hearts. Many of us have looked for love in all the wrong places. We have hoped for prince charming to ride into our lives and make everything bright and beautiful. We have expected our husbands to fill that deep hunger for love within us. We've sought acceptance from other people, believing they could give us value and significance. And over and over, we've been disappointed, because we have expected too much of others. We have looked to people for what only God can do. We have expected our husbands to be like God to us, and all the while, God is deeply, profoundly, hopelessly in love with us. And He's waiting for us to look His way and hear His heart. He's waiting for us to turn aside from the lesser loves of life and to lose ourselves in the experience of His all-consuming, transforming, beautifying love. He's waiting for us to become so rooted and established in the experience of His love for us that we will bear much fruit (see John 15:8). That's who He made us to be—people who bear good fruit, powerful women who know the love of their Father and are walking in their destiny on this earth.

CHAPTER 2

The Love of a King

Since we are destined to be women made alive with the love of our God, we must find out what the love of God looks like. History offers us many ideas of what godlike love is. One of the most famous is found in the mythological Greek goddess of love, Aphrodite, who was so beautiful she was believed to be irresistible. While she was called the goddess of love, she was known as the goddess of sexual rapture. Though married, she continually had affairs with other gods as well as humans. As a normal part of worship in her temple, Aphrodite's priestesses would serve as "stand-ins" for Aphrodite by having sex with her worshippers. In this way, it was said that divine love visited humanity.

In many ways, the story of Aphrodite epitomizes the cultural understanding (both then and now) of divine love. We see it acted out over and over on the movie screen. But does this image of a beautiful and passionate, yet unfaithful and selfish, lover accurately describe the love of God? Many believe this is the ultimate experience of love, yet as Christians, we know true love means so much more. Even the Greeks, though they worshipped Aphrodite, recognized a love much greater than hers.

Ancient Greek, the language of the New Testament, contained four primary words for love—*storgē, eros, phileō,* and *agapē*. In the definitions of these words we find the great variety of meaning encompassed by the single English word *love*. An understanding of these four loves illuminates what God means when He says He loves us—and how that differs from affection for a friend or the love of coffee.

First, let's consider *eros*, or erotic love, the kind of love epitomized in Aphrodite. *Eros* is characterized by overwhelming passion that seizes and absorbs itself in the mind. It is an emotional involvement with another person based on body chemistry, and it is motivated by self-satisfaction. Though this type of love is directed toward another person, it is actually a vehicle of selfishness. A person driven by *eros* believes, "I love you because you make me happy." Because *eros* is based on the pleasure another person brings, when that pleasure ceases, the reason for such love vanishes. Thus, a person may "fall out of love" with another. Simply put, *eros* is motivated by what it can receive, and it gives in order to receive. When expectations go unmet, *eros* can quickly foster bitterness and resentment within a person. The flip side is that those who experience *eros* from others soon learn that being loved is dependent on being attractive or pleasing to another person. It is an earned or conditional love. Not surpris-

Even the Greeks, though they worshipped Aphrodite, recognized a love much greater than hers.

A Love Like That

ingly, though this is our culture's primary definition of romantic love, the word *eros* is completely absent from the New Testament. Contrary to the Greek standard for divine love, *eros* is not how God loves, and it's not how He wants us to love either.

Second is *storgē*, a love most simply defined as "natural affection" or "natural obligation." This natural movement of the soul toward a spouse, child, friend, or pet is based in one's own nature. It is a quiet and abiding feeling within oneself based on something one feels good about. In the New Testament, *storgē* is twice used in the negative form, meaning "unloving" or "without natural affection" (see Rom. 1:31; 2 Tim. 3:3). In both instances, it is used to describe individuals who have given themselves over to sin. They are so far from God that they lack even the *storgē* kind of love. In Romans 12:10, it is combined with *philos* to mean "devoted" or "kindly affectioned," indicating the type of loving devotion we should show toward other believers.

Eros is motivated by what it can receive, and it gives in order to receive.

Third is *phileō*, a companionable love characterized by affection, fondness, or liking. It is awakened in one's heart through positive qualities in others. This is the type of love that responds to kindness, appreciation, or love, and it entails both giving and receiving. It is a higher form of love than *eros*, because it is based on *our* happiness instead of my happiness. However, when the bonds of *phileō* are greatly strained, they can collapse in a crisis. In the New Testament, *phileō* is used multiple times in a positive form (see Matt. 6:5; 10:37; 23:6; 26:48; Mark 14:44; Luke 20:46; 22:47; John 5:20; 11:3, 36; 12:25; 15:19; 16:27; 20:2; 1 Cor. 16:22; Titus 3:15;

Rev. 3:19; 22:15). *Phileō* is also used, in John 21:15–17, to create a contrast between itself and the fourth type of love—*agapē*. We will look at this passage in more depth later.

Forth is *agapē*, the God kind of love. *Agapē* is stirred in one's heart by the great value of the one who is loved. It carries with it the ideas of esteem, evaluation, and prizing. *Agapē* is not based on the merit of the one loved but is rooted in the God-nature within a person. This radical kind of love only originates in God, because it is the embodiment of who He is. When we *agapē*, we are living out the very nature of God that He placed within us. *Agapē* delights in giving, desires only the good of the loved one, and is characterized by a consuming passion for the well-being of others. It keeps on loving, even when the loved one is unresponsive, unkind, unlovable, and unworthy. It is unconditional love.

Though there are only a few known occurrences of *agapē* in non-biblical Greek writings, in the New Testament it appears approximately 320 times. Some of the most notable references include John 3:16, 35; 13:34; 14:15; 15:9, 13; Romans 5:5; 13:8–10; Galatians 5:22; Ephesians 3:17; 4:2, 15; 5:2, 25; Colossians 3:14; First Thessalonians 3:12, 4:9–10; and First Peter 4:8.[2]

In John 21:15–17, we find a vivid contrast between *phileō* and *agapē*. Here is the famous dialogue between Jesus and Peter, when Jesus restored Peter to ministry after he denied Him three times (see Luke 22:54–62). In the text, I have inserted the Greeks words Jesus and Peter used for love:

> *When they had finished eating, Jesus said to Simon Peter, "Simon son of John, do you love [agapē] me more than these?" "Yes, Lord," he said, "you know that I love [phileō] you." Jesus said, "Feed my lambs." Again Jesus said, "Simon*

son of John, do you love [agapē] me?" He answered, "Yes, Lord, you know that I love [phileō] you." Jesus said, "Take care of my sheep." The third time he said to him, "Simon son of John, do you love [phileō] me?" Peter was hurt because Jesus asked him the third time, "Do you love [phileō] me?" He said, "Lord, you know all things; you know that I love [phileō] you." Jesus said, "Feed my sheep" (John 21:15–17).[3]

Twice Jesus asked Peter whether he had *agapē* love for Him, and Peter responded both times acknowledging his *phileō* love for Him. Peter had just denied Jesus three times while Jesus faced death, so we can assume Peter's response here was based on his assessment of his own personal ability to love. He knew he had not done a good job loving Jesus unconditionally, and this is why he grieved when Jesus used *phileō* the third time, seeming to agree with Peter's assessment of himself. Yet in Jesus' final words to him— "*Feed my sheep*"—we can see Peter's redemption. It was as though Jesus said to him, "Even though you don't know how to love with My kind of sacrificial and unconditional love yet, I still trust you and want you to lead My people." Jesus knew Peter would receive and learn to live in *agapē* when he experienced the new birth— and He knows each one of us can, too.

He made us for *agapē*.

CHAPTER 3

Love Has a Face

Agapē love is part of our destiny as daughters of God. It is who He is and who He wants us to be. But before we can learn to give *agapē* to others, we need to receive it from our Father, the King of all. His love is the foundation for transformation from *phileō* to *agapē*, from being people who bear selfish fruit to those who bear selfless fruit. To understand what *agapē* looks like, let's look at the four ways it manifests in God the Father.

1. *Agapé* defines God, expressing the essential nature of who He is.

The first step to understanding *agapē* is realizing that God is the definition of *agapē*. In His character and nature we see what true love really looks like. As the apostle John wrote, *"Whoever does not love does not know God, because God is love"* (1 John 4:8). He didn't say, "God loves," but "God *is* love." He is the source and the meaning of love.

In First Corinthians 13, often called the love chapter, the apostle Paul spelled out for us what this God-love looks like:

> *Love is patient, love is kind. It does not envy, it does not boast, it is not proud. It does not dishonor others, it is not self-seeking, it is not easily angered, it keeps no record of wrongs. Love does not delight in evil but rejoices with the truth. It always protects, always trusts, always hopes, always perseveres. Love never fails* (1 Corinthians 13:4–8a).

This passage is the character section of God's resume. And it rings just as true when we substitute the word *God* for *love*. God is patient, God is kind. He does not envy, He does not boast, He is not proud. He does not dishonor others, He is not self-seeking, He is not easily angered, He keeps no record of wrongs. God does not delight in evil but rejoices with the truth. God always protects, always trusts, always hopes, always perseveres. God never fails. How comforting it is to know that this God called love loves us like this.

2. Agapé defines the Father's attitude toward His Son.

The Trinity—God the Father, Jesus the Son, and the Holy Spirit—is a great big *agapé* party. Each of the members of the Godhead loves the others unconditionally. We see this love within the Trinity in Jesus' declarations: *"The Father loves the Son and has placed everything in his hands"* (John 3:35), and *"For the Father loves the Son and shows him all he does..."* (John 5:20). About His love for the Father, Jesus said, *"I love the Father and do exactly what my Father has commanded me"* (John 14:21). Shortly before He went to the cross, Jesus prayed, *"Father, I want those you have given me to be with me where I am, and to see my glory, the glory you have* given me because you loved me before the creation of the world" (John 17:21). In these passages we see the vibrancy and passion of selfless *agapē* between the Father and the Son.

3. *Agapē* defines the Father's attitude toward humanity.

God's love for humanity is evidenced in His decision to send His Son to make a way for our redemption and restoration to relationship with Him. The most well-known verse of the Bible declares this truth: *"For God so loved the world that he gave his one and only Son, that whoever believes in him shall not perish but have eternal life"* (John 3:16). Though we were hopelessly lost in our sin, God gave of Himself in an incomparable act of *agapē* in order to set us free.

He did this *even while we were still sinners*. That is part of the definition of *agapē*. It keeps on loving, even when the loved one is unresponsive, unkind, unlovable, and unworthy. That was humanity. We had wandered far from our Father, and though our bad choices had hurt Him incredibly, He continued to love us passionately and long for restored relationship with us. This is what the apostle Paul meant when he wrote, *"But God demonstrates his own love for us in this: While we were still sinners, Christ died for us"* (Rom. 5:8). His love for us is truly unconditional, as proven by the fact that He gave everything for us with no guarantee that we would receive the sacrifice He had made. And though many people do not receive the sacrifice, God continues to love all people—*"the world."*

This means, while we were bar-hopping, swinging on a pole, manipulating our kids, cheating at work, or being a "good person," Jesus gave His life for us. This is monumental. It means we don't need to do anything to earn His love. His love for us when we were at our greatest moment of depravity is exactly the same as His love for us at our best moment. That's what *agapē* is all about. We cannot earn it, and it does not change. So many of us, once we become Christians, think we need to perform in order to keep God's love, and we forget what His love is really like. Our God is not *phileō* but *agapē*, and we cannot lose His love.

When we run from Him and reject Him, He doesn't give up on us or come down hard on us. He tenderly woos us back to Himself, back to the perfect peace and joy of His embrace and the destiny on our lives. It is the kindness of His love that calls us to repent, which simply means to turn back around and stop running from our Father (see Rom. 2:4). This kind of crazy love exceeds our human understanding. It's a spiritual revelation.

In Jesus' prayer in John 17, we find an incredible and almost unbelievable statement about the extent of the Father's love for humanity:

> *I have given them the glory that you gave me, that they may be one as we are one—I in them and you in me—so that they may be brought to complete unity. Then the world will know that **you sent me and have loved them even as you have loved me*** (John 17:22–23).

The Father has the same depth of *agapē* love for us as He has for Jesus. This is why He would give His Son to win us back. Jesus would have never given His life for us if we were not worthy of it. That doesn't mean we earned His sacrificial love through our actions. Instead, God appraised us as being valuable enough to Him to deserve the sacrifice. Value is determined by what someone will pay for something. If God paid the life of His Son to redeem our lives, it means our lives are worth that much. His love makes us valuable. When we really understand this, it will completely change our perspective on life and how we relate to our Father. He is so much more committed to us than we know. And we cannot fathom the depths of His love for us.

4. *Agapé* defines the Father's attitude toward those who believe in the Lord Jesus Christ.

The Father doesn't just love us unconditionally while we are sinners, and then, once we return to Him, make us earn His love. Instead, in the act of receiving His *agapé* love into our hearts, we are actually changed to be like Him. We are now *"in Christ"* (Rom. 6:11; 8:1) and empowered to live righteously (see 2 Cor. 5:21). That is what His grace is—divine empowerment to live righteously. Of course, that doesn't mean we are perfect, but it means He sees us according to the sinlessness of Christ. This is why Jesus says, *"Whoever has my commands and keeps them is the one who loves me..."* (John 14:21). It is a statement of fact regarding the power of His love in us to change us. When we reciprocate His love, we begin to be changed into His image from glory to glory (see 2 Cor. 3:18). Keeping His commands is a natural result of abiding in His love. And thus, Jesus continues, *"...The one who loves me will be loved by my Father, and I too will love them and show myself to them"* (John 14:21). In this way, when we accept God's love for us, we are welcomed into the Trinity's *agapé* party.

His love for each one of us is not simple friendship (though it does include that); it is so much more. It is the fiercely burning flame we talked about in the last chapter. His love never abates, never takes a vacation. He is always whispering in our ears, "I love you. I love you. I love you. You are Mine, and I love you. You are precious to Me, and I will never stop loving you." If we stop and listen, we will hear Him. He never stops declaring His love to us in a multitude of ways.

One of the ways He tells me He loves me is through certain parts of His creation that are special to my heart, like butterflies. Whenever I see a butterfly, it is a beautiful little reminder of God's love. It's like He's writing me love notes and hiding them in unexpected places. I'm going along in my day, and suddenly there it is, a little fluttering message of His eternal passion for me. Sometimes I think it's possible God created that butterfly just for me. He loves to send me little surprises as reminders of His love—like a husband might send his wife flowers.

Once, a few years ago, He wowed me with a surprise that illustrates this point so clearly. My husband and I have been supporters of Joyce Meyer Ministries for several years, and prior to her seventieth birthday, I received a handwritten note from her office to all her partners about a surprise they wanted to do for her birthday. The note invited each of us to write Joyce a note for her birthday, telling her how she had impacted our lives. As I read the note, I thought, *What a wonderful idea!* Then I thought, *Wow, with all the partners they have, Joyce will probably receive countless responses. I would rather tell her in person what she means to me and my family and how her teaching ministry has impacted us.*

Throughout my children's junior high and high school years, every morning at 7 a.m. I would turn the TV to her program, "Enjoying Everyday Life." My children would eat breakfast, and I would make their school lunches as we listened to her teach us about Jesus, who we are in Christ, and so many other practical teachings about how to live and enjoy everyday life. As a mom, I have no greater joy than seeing my children hear the truth of

God's word! Joyce Meyer played a large part in making that a daily reality for my kids during very formative years. Her messages were always positive, practical, and biblically sound, and I felt a lot of gratitude for her and her ministry.

Not long after I received that letter about Joyce Meyer's birthday surprise, I was in Florida for a writing and praying retreat, as is my custom. While there, each morning I workout at a gym and afterward get my morning coffee. One morning, I decided to try out a new gym I'd found online, but I had a very difficult time finding it. I ended up back tracking several times because the GPS kept directing me to the wrong place. Eventually, I gave up and decided to just go get my coffee. On the way, I heard the Lord say to me, "I have something special planned for you today." I thought, *OK, that was an interesting thing for Him to say.*

When we run from Him and reject Him, He doesn't give up on us.

When I finally arrived at my favorite coffee shop, I stood in line waiting to order my coffee. Suddenly, I heard a very distinct and familiar voice. I looked over to my right, and there was Joyce Meyer having coffee with another woman. So after I ordered my coffee, I went up to her, first apologizing for being rude and intrusive. She looked up at me, smiled, and kindly said, "It's OK." Quickly, I told her how thankful I am for her ministry and the tremendous impact she has had on my family.

When I walked away, I smiled to myself. All the back tracking and what I had thought was wasted time in the car had really been a set up from God to cause me to arrive at the right place at the right time so He could surprise me by giving me the desire of my heart. He loves to do the same for all of us, because He doesn't play favorites (see Acts 10:34). He is on a mission to convince each one of us of the depth of His love for us so we can experience His fullness.

That's what He wants. He doesn't want us to walk around life defining ourselves by the standards of *eros* or *storgē* or even *phileō*. He doesn't want us to think we need to perform well in order to be special or valuable. When we think like that, we have a hard time loving ourselves, because we think our legs aren't as nice as someone's or our bust size is too small or our personality is too introverted—and the list goes on. God doesn't want us hating on ourselves like that, because He made us and loves us as we are. We are beautiful and valuable *because He says so.* Who better understands the worth of something than the one who created it? We need to take Him at His word. He is our creator, and He says we are valuable and important and captivating. And He loves us no matter what, forever and always.

CHAPTER 4

When Love Came Down

Talking about God as a God of love can raise a lot of questions. People read the Old Testament and wonder how the God depicted there can be the Father God Jesus talked about in the New Testament. How can the God of the Flood and the plagues and many wars be a God of love? While I can't sufficiently address that question in this book, I hope to provide the beginning of an answer.[4]

The truth is, God the Father has always loved humanity. In the Old Testament, His heart comes through in His continual wooing of His people, calling them back again and again though they had turned their backs on Him. Ultimately, because sin had so clouded human hearts, people had a very hard time loving God. Sometimes they feared Him or revered Him, but very rarely did they really love Him. And that, of course, has been His desire since He created Adam and Eve as His companions in the Garden of Eden.

So to win His people back, God decided to not only forgive their sins through a radical atonement sacrifice but also to empower them with the ability to love Him back. This is what Jesus came to do. This is why love came down to earth and lived and died among us. In Christ, we see the full manifestation of God's love for us. Though during Old Testament times the fullness of His love was hidden in a mystery, through Jesus it was revealed (see 1 Cor. 2:6–10). Yet the apostle Paul says of this manifestation of God's love and wisdom:

> *What we have received is not the spirit of the world, but the Spirit who is from God, so that we may understand what God has freely given us. This is what we speak, not in words taught us by human wisdom but in words taught by the Spirit, explaining spiritual realities with Spirit-taught words. The person without the Spirit does not accept the things that come from the Spirit of God but considers them foolishness, and cannot understand them because they are discerned only through the Spirit (1 Corinthians 2:12–14).*

In other words, apart from the Spirit, we cannot possibly understand God's wisdom in sending Jesus to earth to die for our sins. It is crazy love. But when the Spirit lives inside us, we can begin to grasp the absolute wisdom of God's extravagant decision to give Himself to win back our love. With this in mind, let's consider how Jesus manifested the love of God for humanity through both His life on earth and His death on the cross.

Before Jesus was born on earth, He existed eternally with the Father in Heaven. We see this in Jesus' statement: *"No one has ever gone into heaven except the one who came from heaven—the Son of*

Man" (John 3:13). He also said, *"I am the living bread that came down from heaven. Whoever eats this bread will live forever. This bread is my flesh, which I will give for the life of the world"* (John 6:51). Jesus left Heaven to rescue us. He left the perfect *agapē* party of the Trinity and came down among His creation, many of whom despised Him.

Leaving Heaven was obviously a great sacrifice, yet Jesus chose to do it because of His desire to manifest to the world the fullness of who the Father is and His heart for humanity. As John writes, *"And the Word became flesh and dwelt among us, and we beheld His glory, the glory as of the only begotten of the Father, full of grace and truth"* (John 1:14). Through Jesus, we see the glory of God, and we are invited to share in His glory as children and heirs of God (see Rom. 8:17). Christ sacrificed Heaven so that the glory of God displayed in Him might enable His glory to shine in our hearts:

> *For God, who said, "Let light shine out of darkness," made his light shine in our hearts to give us the light of the knowledge of God's glory displayed in the face of Christ (2 Corinthians 4:6).*

Not only did Jesus come in love, but He lived in love and ministered with great compassion. The apostle Peter's description of Jesus' earthly ministry highlights His many acts of compassion:

> *God anointed Jesus of Nazareth with the Holy Spirit and with power, who went about doing good and healing all who were oppressed by the devil, for God was with Him (Acts 10:38).*

This was the dominant thrust of His ministry. Yes, He called people to repentance and righteousness and condemned the hypocrisy of the Pharisees and scribes. Yes, He prophesied coming judgment against those who rejected Him. Yet His main focus was on simple belief in and love for God. And He demonstrated how good and kind and loving God really is by pursuing and caring for the poor and broken and needy. In fact, He cited this sort of ministry as the very evidence of His identity as the Messiah. When John the Baptist sent some of his disciples to ask Jesus if He was indeed the Messiah, Jesus replied:

> Go back and report to John what you hear and see: The blind receive sight, the lame walk, those who have leprosy are cleansed, the deaf hear, the dead are raised, and the good news is proclaimed to the poor (Matthew 11:4–5).

In other words, acts of love and compassion for all, including the "least" of society, was proof Jesus was from God, because such acts are in God's heart. Isaiah had prophesied the Messiah would be a man of compassion and healing, and Jesus read Isaiah's words at the beginning of His earthly ministry:

> The Spirit of the Lord is on me, because he has anointed me to proclaim good news to the poor. He has sent me to proclaim freedom for the prisoners and recovery of sight for the blind, to set the oppressed free, to proclaim the year of the Lord's favor (Luke 4:18–19).

Then He declared, "Today this scripture is fulfilled in your hearing" (Luke 4:21). Here He plainly states these acts of compassion were motivated by the will of the Father. In fact, Jesus made it clear He was motivated by the Father in everything He did. He said, *"Very truly I tell you, the Son can do nothing by himself; he can do only what he sees his Father doing, because whatever the Father does the Son also does"* (John 5:19). And in passage after passage, we see Jesus respond to people in compassion. In this, Jesus was not acting in compassion apart from the Father. Instead, He was manifesting the Father's own compassionate heart of love for all people.

Some people think of Jesus as being the compassionate one who protects us from God's wrath, but that is not scriptural. He did not come to protect humanity from an angry God but to show humanity who God really is and the truth of His heart toward us. He came to remind us that God is *"compassionate and gracious, slow to anger, abounding in love"* (Ps. 103:8). He has always been moved by love and compassion.

With this in mind, it makes sense that Jesus, who only did what He saw His Father do, was continually moved by compassion. When He saw the multitudes, who were *"weary and scattered, like sheep having no shepherd,"* He was moved by compassion (Matt. 9:36). His compassion wasn't just a sympathetic feeling; it caused Him to take action, to heal their sick (see Matt. 14:14) and multiply food for them (see Matt. 15:32). When He encountered the outcasts of society—the blind, the lepers, the demon possessed, even the dead—His compassion caused Him to reach out and touch them with the Father's love (see Matt. 20:34; Mark 1:41; 9:22; Luke 7:12–14). And they were all healed. In fact, according to Finis Jennings Dake, the Bible commentator, "Never is there a case recorded where Jesus failed to have compassion. His compassion through the work of the Holy Spirit had power over death."[5]

Near the end of His life on earth, Jesus prayed to His Father: *"I have made you known to them, and will continue to make you known in order that the love you have for me may be in them and that I myself may be in them*" (John 17:26). He had accomplished the first part of His mission on earth—to make the Father known through a life of radical compassion and undeserved love. Now He was ready for the second part—the culmination of all His acts of love in His death on the cross.

When Jesus, the sinless Son of God, became the final sacrifice to atone for our sin nature, He paid the ultimate price to demonstrate God's crazy love for humanity. He allowed Himself to be betrayed by a friend, to be beaten by an angry mob comprised of people He loved, to be whipped and deformed by those He had lovingly created, and to be nailed to a cross for those He valued more than His own life. And He did it all for love. Paul describes the great heart of Jesus this way:

> *Who, being in very nature God, did not consider equality with God something to be used to his own advantage; rather, he made himself nothing by taking the very nature of a servant, being made in human likeness. And being found in appearance as a man, he humbled himself by becoming obedient to death— even death on a cross* (Philippians 2:6–8).

Because of this great love sacrifice, the Father has exalted Jesus to the *"highest place"* (Phil. 2:9). Only such radical embodiment of the Father's love gave Christ the highest place of honor. That is how much the Father values love for humanity.

And when Jesus rose from the dead, He invited all of us back into relationship with God, not on our own merit but on His. Because He loved us, He earned our place for us. *"For by grace you have been saved through faith, and that not of yourselves; it is the gift of God"* (Eph. 2:8). The power of such love is incomprehensible. Truly it is stronger than death. And because of this great act of

A Love Like That

love, not only may we now experience intimate relationship with God and joy and victory in our lives on earth, but one day we will live eternally in Heaven with God. As the popular worship song declares:

> Love came down and rescued me.
> Love came down and set me free.
> I am Yours.
> I am forever Yours.[6]

CHAPTER 5

Freed to Fly

When loves comes down and sets us free, we are changed. Encountering His love, we are transformed into a new creation. A page turns, and a new chapter begins. *"The old has gone, the new is here!"* (2 Cor. 5:17). We can never be the same again, because when God sets us free with His love, we are free indeed (see John 8:36). We are like the caterpillar who metamorphoses into a butterfly. Suddenly we have wings, and we are freed to fly.

My own experience of transformation from death into life through the power of Christ's love happened when I was nineteen years old. For the first time, I encountered His love, and in that moment, everything changed. I was born again (see John 3:3; 1 Pet. 1:23). Even my best friend from high school attested to the stark change in me. In a recent conversation, reflecting on those days, she said, "One day you were one way, and the next day you were radically different, and I didn't know what to do with you."

Here's how it happened for me. All my life I was hungry for God.

I wanted to know His heart and know the love He had for me. I grew up Catholic, went to a Catholic private school, and absolutely loved it. In the Catholic Church, I learned about the saints and Mary the mother of God. I had an altar in my room with fresh flowers, and at this altar I would pray to Mary (I know now that is unbiblical). Every night I would pray the rosary and hide it under my pillow. At my school, we were required to attend church every morning, and we also had a religion class. I loved anything to do with knowing God and His love for me, but I had no idea how to find God. I felt like I was still disconnected from His love, and I didn't know why.

In the Catholic Church, they taught me Jesus was still on the cross and I needed to confess my sins to a priest. No one ever told me I needed to believe in Jesus and accept Him into my heart. No one ever talked about being born again. Instead, they talked about church. That, I was told, was the place where one would meet God. Though the truth of salvation is clearly spelled out in the Bible, no one ever told me:

> If you declare with your mouth, "Jesus is Lord," and believe in your heart that God raised him from the dead, you will be saved. For it is with your heart that you believe and are justified, and it is with your mouth that you profess your faith and are saved (Romans 10:9–10).

I didn't know what a prayer of salvation was or that simply by believing in Jesus I could receive salvation and full relationship with God. I had no idea. But I had this heart tug and longing for love. I was searching for God while partying every weekend and hanging out with my friends. And I couldn't find Him anywhere.

Though I was clueless about God, every night I would talk to Him. I would ask Him to show Himself to me. Ever since I was a little girl, sitting on a tree stump in our back yard and looking up into the big, blue, extravagant sky, I had wanted to see His face. I would call out, "God, I want to see Your face!"—hoping with everything in me His face would appear in the sky, and I would get to see Him.

When I was confirmed in the Catholic Church, I took it very seriously. And during the ceremony, for the first time in my life, I felt the tangible presence of the Holy Spirit come upon me. As I sat there being bathed by the most amazing feeling I had ever encountered, all the other children were talking and laughing in their seats. He was so very real to me, I could not understand why no one else felt Him there with us. The feeling of His presence lasted for three days. When it left, I felt an even greater desire to know God.

During my childhood, I spent a lot of time alone, talking to God. I loved Him with all of my heart and soul. The uncertainties of my home life caused me a lot of anxiety, but I would pray to God and ask Him to help me cope, and He always came through for me. My whole childhood was filled with a precious communion with God, and I went to Him for everything. Because my parents were not emotionally available for me, I learned to run to Him as my Father. I always enjoyed being with Him, and I talked to Him about everything.

Yet in a very real sense, I did not know who God was. I related to Him through my simple, childlike faith and the purity of my heart, but I did not have any understanding. I didn't know He could live in my heart. This is why I cried out to see His face, why I wanted Heaven to open and reveal the truth of who He is. Deep inside, I knew there must be more, but I didn't know how to find it. I had spent my whole life longing for Heaven to come down to me. I didn't know it then, but God puts this desire to know Him, this desire to be deeply and intimately acquainted with Him, in all His children.

When I was a child, God began to reveal Himself to me, but I didn't have anyone to teach me, and the teaching I did receive in my Catholic education only hid the truth of salvation from me. Because of this lack of revelation about God, during my teen years, I stepped back from God and embraced the party scene, hoping to find the love I longed for. One day, while working in a factory cutting excess plastic from blue hermetic coils, I decided I didn't want to be wholeheartedly committed to God anymore. My season of childhood innocence and faith had ended, I had reached the age of accountability, and I made a choice against God. As the Bible says, *"...Sin sprang to life and I died* [spiritually]" (Romans 7:9).

That was not a very happy season. I had no direction for my life but instead spent my time partying with my friends. Though my mother took me to visit colleges, I had no interest in going. I was floundering and visionless. I didn't know what I wanted to do. During those years, God still pursued my heart, reminding me of the experiences I had with Him as a child. At times, as I drove in my car, a love song would come on the radio, and I would feel the conviction of the Holy Spirit in the song, even though it was a secular love song about a man and a woman. He was calling me to Himself, reminding me that He had a plan for my aimless life. But I didn't know how to be saved or even what it meant to be saved. I felt frustrated and confused, and so for a season I stubbornly refused to listen to His calling.

As the tug of God's conviction grew, so did my unhappiness. I felt the pull of the two worlds, the fight for my life between good and evil. One night, as I drove down the highway, this struggle seemed so real to me. I could feel the pull from the Holy Spirit and the pull from the forces of darkness. They both wanted my life. This realization shook me up, and I began to pray again when alone in my room. I asked Him to help. I asked Him to show me His heart. I asked Him to save me, not even knowing what that meant. I prayed like that for a whole year.

I was empty and unhappy, and I wanted to know my purpose. I knew life must contain more than what I was experiencing. So night after night, I prayed and cried out to Him. I found an old Catholic Bible on a bookshelf at my home, and I randomly began to read from the book of Psalms. No one had ever told me to read the Psalms, but the Holy Spirit was working in me and gently guiding me toward the truth, even though I didn't realize it (see John 16:7–11).

My season of... faith had ended, I made a choice against God.

Then one night, after I had cleaned up my room, I cried out to God as I had been for the last year, "I just want to know You! I don't understand, but I just want You. What must I do to be saved? I have done everything I know to do, and I'm still not saved. Please, I want to know you and be close to You. *What must I do to be saved?*" But this time was different, because as I sat there alone, I heard something. I heard God answer from deep inside me, in the chambers of my heart. For the first time in my life, I heard the audible, authoritative voice of God. In a deep, comforting voice, He said to me, "Only believe." And that was it. That was what I needed.

Suddenly, I understood, and faith arose in my heart. Aloud I declared, "I believe!" At that moment, light turned on in my heart. I felt the power of darkness lift off me, and for the first time in my life I felt true love, the *agapē* love of my Father. It was like nothing I had ever known before. It was so much deeper and stronger than what I had experienced of Him as a child. It seemed as though the whole room had lit up and was glowing with His presence and the throb of His love for me. Suddenly His peace and love like no other were pouring into my heart, and I was born again into the Spirit. I was transformed in a moment by His consuming love. At last, I had found my Father, and He had made me whole.

From that moment on, everything in my life changed. The next day I went to my parents and hugged them, telling them about my experience of being born again. It was foreign to them, even though my mother had been involved with the Catholic charismatic movement and had always been committed to her church. This was a new level of experience for them, but they were supportive. As it turns out, they had been praying for me. And God had answered their prayers by bringing me back to Himself and showing me how to be saved.

> *At last, I had found my Father, and He had made me whole.*

Six months later, in July of 1976, I was on my way to Bible school, where I learned all about God, the Bible, and prayer. A few months after I finished Bible school, my desire for more of God increased immensely, and though I was already filled with the Holy Spirit and spoke with other tongues, I found myself feeling dissatisfied in my new relationship with Christ. *What could this be?* I thought. In that season, Psalm 63:1–2 became my heart's cry to the Father.

> *You, God, are my God, earnestly I seek you; I thirst for you, my whole being longs for you, in a dry and parched land where there is no water. I have seen you in the sanctuary and beheld your power and your glory.*

I had learned the Scriptures and theology in this amazing Bible school, and now God, by way of the Holy Spirit, began to expand my prayer life so I eventually could see the world through His eyes. In my prayer closet, He showed me the needs of other people and how He longs to meet them. He showed me cities and nations in need of revival and the strongholds over them, keeping them from His glory. And what I saw affected my heart! As I yielded myself to the Holy Spirit, I found myself crying out on behalf of these people, cities, and nations. I was in tears for the lost. At times, the burden of the Lord moved so strongly in me that I thought my heart would break.

One day, in the midst of this season, God told me, if I would totally yield to Him, He would use me as an instrument to accomplish His will on earth, and Jesus the great intercessor would move sovereignly through me. He also told me intercessory prayer will be the key to one of the mightiest revivals the earth will ever see. "There is a great need for this kind of praying in the body of Christ," He told me, "And I am searching for intercessors who will stand in the gap for people, ministries, cities, and nations."

I said, "Here I am, Lord! Flow through me."

Soon after, in 1981, I began to travel and speak full time all over the East Coast. In many churches, I was the first woman to ever preach. As I followed His lead, the Holy Spirit did amazing things in those meetings. Many people were saved, healed, and called into the work of the ministry. Together, God and I had a lot of fun! I was discovering that God's plans for my life were truly amazing and fulfilling. Life with Him, surrounded by His love, was better than I had ever imagined it could be, and this was only the beginning.

I am so thankful God reached down into my life when I felt no hope, saved me from myself, and gave me a life worth living. Truly, when He sets us free by the power of His love, we are free indeed.

If you have not yet accepted Jesus into your heart as your Lord and Savior, I invite you to do so now. He loves you more than you will ever know, and He longs for you to return to Him and to experience the fullness and safety of His love. Jesus already died on the cross and rose again to purchase your salvation from sin and freedom into new life. All you need to do is believe He did it and accept His sacrifice. It is as simple as my declaration as a nineteen-year-old: "I believe!" As you do, His Spirit will come into your heart, and you will be changed.

Here is a simple prayer you can pray:

Father God, I know You love me. You loved me so much You sent Your Son to die on the cross for me. Today I accept into my heart the reality of this sacrifice. I believe Jesus died on the cross for me and then rose from the dead. Jesus, I am asking You to come into my heart. I now make You the Lord of my life.

CHAPTER 6

On the Road with Love

When we encounter the love of God and are changed in His presence, we begin an amazing journey. But it is only the beginning. According to the Bible, we are instantly changed when we accept Christ into our hearts, and we continue to change, to "grow up" in Christ throughout our lives. We exist in a dual reality. We are spiritually transformed into a new creation. In Christ, our old selves died, and our new selves were born (see Rom. 6:6–7). Yet the apostle Peter, writing to believers, made clear our responsibility to pursue maturity: *"Like newborn babies, crave pure spiritual milk, so that by it you may grow up in your salvation"* (1 Pet. 2:2). In other words, becoming a new creation does not mean instant perfection. While we live on earth, we continue to experience the maturation process, even though in Christ we have been made perfect. Hebrews 10:14 sums this up perfectly: *"For by one sacrifice **he has made perfect** forever those who **are being made holy***" (Heb. 10:14).

This process of transformation is worked out in our lives through a continual submitting to our Father and through daily encountering and living in His love. It's not about striving to make ourselves perfect but about allowing Him to work His character and nature into us. It is like what happens with a potter and clay.

This illustration makes sense to me, especially since I work with ceramics. As a potter, I can take a little piece of clay and make it into a pot. Each pot I make is uniquely fashioned and beautiful, and each has its own name. When it comes to transformation, God is our potter: *"Yet you, Lord, are our Father. We are the clay, you are the **potter**; we are all the work of your hand"* (Isa. 64:8). He molds and shapes us tenderly with His hands.

Simply put, *transformation* is the continual process of understanding and knowing the love of God and allowing that love to change us. This is why the apostle Paul described it as the renewing of our minds:

> *Do not conform to the pattern of this world, but be transformed by the renewing of your mind. Then you will be able to test and approve what God's will is—his good, pleasing and perfect will* (Romans 12:2).

When we are saved into the Kingdom of light, our spirits are instantly transformed into righteousness, but our minds still need some convincing. This is what it means to be transformed, to receive the mind of Christ so we can live out the new nature He has given us. I like to tell my kids, "Life is a journey, not a race." In other words, we need to be patient. We need to rest in God's love and allow Him to work in us, trusting that *"he who began a good work in you will carry it on to completion..."* (Phil. 1:6). As we do,

He will continually be working change in our lives as we journey along the road of life with Him.

I am not the same person I was when I was born again at the age of nineteen. I know what it's like to be one person and to be transformed and molded into another person, to still be myself, but the God version of myself. I am being transformed. And I am not the same person I was even a year ago. Year after year, day after day, His love is changing me. The Bible says we progress from glory to glory and from faith to faith:

> But we all, with unveiled face, beholding as in a mirror the glory of the Lord, are being transformed into the same image from glory to glory, just as by the Spirit of the Lord (2 Corinthians 3:18 NKJV).

> For in it [the gospel of Christ] the righteousness of God is revealed from faith to faith; as it is written, "The just shall live by faith" (Romans 1:17).

His love is transforming us. If we embrace that process with patience, He will do amazing things in and through us. I know this from personal experience. Often, we are blind to the extent of our need for transformation. We think we are ready for the fullness of our destiny right now, but in His love, God pulls us back and takes us through a refining process so we can truly excel in all He's called us to do. For me, one of the most significant seasons of refining and mind-renewing was motherhood.

I had already been in ministry for four years when I married my husband, John. After being married and continuing in ministry for another five years, we decided to have children. When we had trouble conceiving, we sought professional help, and I was able to conceive through in vitro fertilization. Our twins, Jonathan and Danielle, were born at thirty weeks, and we were so thankful. As preemies, they had to stay in the hospital for the first six weeks, but when they finally came home, they were healthy and full of life. Seven months after the twins were born, I discovered I was already twenty weeks pregnant, and nineteen weeks later, I gave birth to another daughter, Jaclyn. Suddenly, within the span of one year, 1992, I had birthed three children, and life would never be the same again.

I loved being the mother of three babies. Truly, it was one of the happiest seasons of my life. It was also the beginning of an intense season of hiddenness—spanning the next eighteen years—in which God transformed me and prepared me for the later part of my calling to ministry. During those years, I stepped back from ministry and focused on my role as wife and mother.

Year after year, day after day, His love is changing me.

I fed babies, changed diapers, and planned play dates. And all the while, God was training me.

One winter I bought three small tricycles to occupy my three toddlers indoors. Atop these, they raced around and around on our cream tile floors. Once, as Jonathan came around a corner on his tricycle and asked me for a cookie, I heard the Holy Spirit say, "There is a need for My Church to pray."

I looked around at my three young children and said to Him, "What do You want me to do?" It didn't seem like I could do anything right then, but the call of God remained. While I was on hold from public ministry, God was training me to reach the next generation. I didn't realize it at the time, but as I raised my own children, He was equipping me to raise and train the next generation of leaders. I was receiving inside information on what was going on with our young people—the tests, trials, and strategies of the enemy designed to take out this next generation.

When the twins were in fifth grade and Jaclyn was in fourth grade, God drew me back into the prayer closet. I would put the kids on the bus, go into my office, and spend time with God. I rarely went shopping and hardly had a social life. All I wanted was to get close to God. I call this season of my life the time when I was "hidden in the house." It was a time of preparation and refinement, when God spoke to me about living in the light of eternity. I spent hours studying the Scriptures, praying, listening to teaching tapes, and reading books. I was clay on the great potter's wheel, and He was reworking me completely. On and on and on the wheel spun, and over the course of years the new, transformed me was taking shape.

All I wanted was to get close to God.

As the kids continued to grow, I entered the chauffer mom stage, spending six or more hours in the car driving them back and forth to school and their various activities, as well as several more hours a week waiting in parking lots during hockey or dance practices. I knew I was in preparation for public ministry, so instead of wasting time, I listened to hours and hours of teaching tapes in the car. God was speaking to me, strengthening me emotionally, and reassuring me of His love, care, and approval. He was building my confidence in Him to make me ready for the years of ministry to come.

Once all three kids went to college, God released me to once again run full-time in ministry. While I am so excited for what is ahead, I am also incredibly thankful for what God has taken me through and the years of refining and transforming. Truly, those years of being hidden in God's love have made me who I am. This progressive transformation in the love of God is a process we all need to experience. God loves us so much He is not content to let us believe the lies our enemy has told us, because these lies hold us back from abundant life and keep us from being able to fully receive God's love for us.

Without this transformation process, we will never become who He has made us to be. Of course, God uniquely tailors this transformation journey for each one of us. No two experiences are exactly alike, but the bottom line is the same. As we behold His face, we are transformed into His image from glory to glory (see 2 Cor. 3:18). As we allow God to renew our minds—to change the way we think about our lives, about ourselves, and about Him— we are transformed into His image (see Rom. 12:2).

In the remainder of this book, I will address two primary ways in which God's transformation happens in our lives.

First, transformation happens as we hear and accept what God says about us. Many of us have believed lies about ourselves because of our life experiences and the ways other people have treated us. God wants to heal the wounds of these experiences and give us a new lens (His lens) to view ourselves through. We will address this in Part 2: "Changed by His Love."

Second, transformation happens as we develop an intimate love relationship with God. It is the power of His love that changes us, and the more we experience His love, the more we are changed into His image. The more we look into His face, the more we look like Him. This is the topic of Part 3: "Continuing in His Love."

This is how we walk with Love along the road of our lives—how He changes us completely, burning out the old and ugly and painful and filling us with His peace and joy and beauty. This is how we daughters come to look very much like our Father, walking arm-in-arm with Him.

A Love Like That

PART 2

Changed by
His Love

*P*sychology teaches us that our self-concept, or how we think and feel about ourselves, is developed by how the most important people in our lives view us. In other words, the way the most important people in our lives view us and treat us, as well as what we think about how they view and treat us, determines how we view ourselves. We are shaped by the opinions of others, especially in our childhood. Unfortunately, for many of us, such shaping has not had a positive effect. The good news is, when God comes into our lives and takes that place of "most important person," He will completely change our self-concept. When we see ourselves the way He sees us, we realize how amazing we really are, and we are empowered to overcome the difficulties of life.

Most people simply accept and believe everything the most important people in their lives say about them. And they absorb messages about their own value from how those people treat them. That's how God created us to be—we understand who we are in relationship to the most important person in our lives. In His original design, that person is Him. We need Him to fill that void of meaning and value, to tell us what we're worth and how loved we are. Without that, we are easy prey for the enemy. And we quickly become the emotional victims of other wounded people who have never experienced true love. When we are not filled up with the knowledge of who we are in Christ, it is very difficult to resist and refuse to believe some of the things people have said about us.

But when we encounter God's love and are changed in His presence, we no longer have to accept the lies of the enemy. We don't have to believe what people have said about us. We only have to believe what He says. He becomes our lie detector, our truthful witness. When we know who God our Father is and who we are in Him, we will be able to confidently believe we are not who those negative voices have said we are. We will care only for God's opinion.

To that end, in Part 2 of this book, I am going to look at how our understanding of who God is and how He views us has the power to completely transform our self-image and, therefore, our lives. In the next seven chapters, we will look at how God renews our minds and the way we see ourselves in order to help us:

- benefit from hard times
- forgive those who've hurt us
- receive healing from childhood wounds
- stand-up to abuse and oppression
- hear what God says about us

Get ready to have your mind transformed by the revelation of who your Father is and what He says about you.

CHAPTER 7

Through Fire and Water

When I was in my early twenties, I traveled with a friend of mine, Stephanie Boosahda, who is a singer and songwriter. During the course of our trip, she was featured as a guest on TBN (Trinity Broadcasting Network), along with the prophet Dick Mills. Afterward, as we were riding back to the hotel with Dick Mills, he turned to me and said, "You're going to go through the fire, and you're going to go through water." He quoted Psalm 66:12, which says, *"You let people ride over our heads; we went through fire and water, but you brought us to a place of abundance."* Then he said, "You are going to be able to comfort people who have had problems with rejection, betrayal, divorce, sexual abuse"—all because I was essentially going to go through hell. He told me I would be betrayed by my brothers, like Joseph, and that they would speak all kinds of evil against me. And in the end, God wanted me to forgive them.

I thought to myself, sarcastically, *What a wonderful prophecy! Thanks for that!*

But it all happened just like he said it would (I'll tell you about it in the next chapter). I went through fire and water and experienced betrayal from those closest to me, but in the end, God redeemed it all. He renewed my mind to enable me to forgive and to see His goodness in the midst of the pain. Psalm 66 describes my experience well: *"You let people ride over our heads; we went through fire and water, but you brought us to a place of abundance"* (Ps. 66:12). He transformed me into an overcomer.

> *Our trials don't have to make us bitter.*

Through this experience, I learned in a very real way that the devil hates me. In fact, he hates all of us simply because we are made in the image of God. He wants to steal the anointing on our lives and prevent us from finding peace and joy in God. Especially when he sees God beginning to do a new thing in our lives, the enemy tries to sabotage it by bringing in trials and difficulties. He tries to mess with us and get us to give up or get angry or bitter.

But our trials don't have to make us bitter. In fact, by the grace of God, they should make us better. Some of the difficulties we go through are preparation for our calling. Embedded in them are important lessons for us, lessons we need in order to succeed. The psalmist described it this way: *"Praise be to the Lord my Rock, who trains my hands for war, my fingers for battle"* (Ps. 144:1). But our ability to learn these lessons and receive His training is dependent on our attitude. If we mope and complain, saying, "Why do I have to go through this? Why is this happening to me?" we risk missing out on the goodness of God hidden in our difficulties.

At times, God allows us to go through difficult times. At other times, these difficulties are attacks from the enemy. But the good news is that God triumphs in them all. Every difficulty we face, no matter its source, can be turned to our benefit if we keep our hearts open to God and continue to trust Him. As Paul wrote, *"And we know that in all things God works for the good of those who love him, who have been called according to his purpose"* (Rom. 8:28). When our hearts are secure in God's love and we don't begin to question Him or become angry or bitter about our circumstances, God will always find a way to redeem our pain and struggle. He will renew our minds to see the good He is doing in our hearts through the process, and He will enable us to see our circumstances with His eternal perspective. He is that good and that loving.

The key to experiencing the redemption He has for us in all circumstances is abiding in His love and staying obedient to His Word. When we do that, He will be able to renew our minds with His understanding. Jesus told a parable about the impact difficulty can have on our lives by comparing two men and the houses they built. The wise man built his house on the rock—Jesus—and so was able to weather the storm. But the foolish man built his house on the sand, and when the storm came, his house was consumed (see Matt. 7:24–27). In other words, if we build the foundation of our lives on God's love for us and our relationship with Him, nothing in this life will be able to destroy us. No matter what storms may come, He will hold us steady. But if our lives are built on the shifting sands of life and circumstances, we will be easily devastated by the storms of life.

> *If our lives are built on the shifting sands of life and circumstances, we will be easily devastated...*

It is not always easy to keep our heads above the storm. Sometimes life feels very overwhelming, and we get tired. We give in, and we put down our swords. We stop fighting for God's truth in our lives, and we start believing some of the devil's lies about ourselves and how hopeless or pitiful our lives are. I know this, because I've been there. *"The rain came down, the streams rose, and the winds blew and beat against [my] house"* (Matt. 7:27), and I got tired.

I had three kids in one year, and four years later, I got really tired. I didn't sleep through the night for four years straight. Then my mother and my father died within six weeks of each other. And then we moved to a new community where I had no friends. Every time I went up the road to our new house, I felt like no one wanted us to be there. At the time, I didn't realize I was discerning in the spirit and these feelings were a spiritual attack against me. If I had listened to the warning from the Holy Spirit and fortified myself by listening to solid Bible teaching, by listening to the audio Bible while making dinner, or playing worship music in the house, I would have found the strength I needed. If I had allowed Him to renew my mind in that situation, I would have understood what was happening and known how to fight back in the spirit, but I was too tired to listen.

We all have experienced seasons like this. We have all experienced the temptation to give in to tiredness, to be overwhelmed. But we don't have to give in, and we don't have to stay there. God has promised He will not allow us to be tempted beyond what we can bear. He will not allow the enemy to overwhelm us.

> *No temptation has overtaken you except what is common to mankind. And God is faithful; he will not let you be tempted beyond what you can bear. But when you are tempted,*

he will also provide a way out so that you can endure it
(1 Corinthians 10:13).

When we stay close to the Father's heart and allow Him to continually renew our minds to His way of thinking, we will not be overcome. Instead, we will overcome. And we will sharpen our swords on the struggles of life. We will use them to our advantage, because we will have the mind of Christ and see from Heaven's perspective. That is our way of escape—the renewing of our minds so we can perceive as He does. When we allow Him to renew our minds, God can use all our circumstances to teach and train us in faith and righteousness. He will take the pain of our struggles and shape it into tools we can use to help others.

We won't be taken out; we'll be transformed by the knowledge of who He says we are as the new creation:

> *I do not pray that You should take them out of the world, but that You should **keep them from the evil one**. They are not of the world, just as I am **not of the world*** (John 17:15–16).

When we realize we are not of this world, but above it, seated with Christ in heavenly places (see Eph. 2:6), we are able to overcome. In this way, our attitude does determine our altitude. If we decide to agree with the mind of Christ and allow Him to renew our minds, we will rise above our circumstances. But if we get stuck in our human reasoning and questions, we will be weighed down under our circumstances. The choice is always ours. If we choose the high road, we will come through our circumstances with a testimony of God's goodness and love for us and a greater revelation of the faith that overcomes.

This is why T.D. Jakes can say, "To all my enemies—you did me a favor."[7] He says this because he truly believes God will use all difficulties for our good when we trust Him. He believes what Paul wrote about this in Second Corinthians 1:4:

> *Praise be to the God and Father of our Lord Jesus Christ, the Father of compassion and the God of all comfort, who comforts us in all our tribulation, **that we may be able to comfort those who are in any trouble,** with the comfort with which we ourselves are comforted by God.*

In other words, when we go through hard times, we are equipped to help others when they go through hard times. The devil thinks he knows what he is doing, but when we are planted firmly on the rock, his attacks only make us stronger and more effective in ministry to others. When we allow God to renew our minds, He really can redeem our struggles by enabling us to minister more effectively to others. God is not a mean God. He is not causing the struggles in our lives. That's the devil. And sometimes we cause them ourselves through our own foolishness. But God is always good, and He always gives good gifts to His children (see James 1:17). His love for us is so strong that He grieves with us and comforts us in our pain, and He also finds a way to bring something good from it.

All this doesn't mean our struggles don't hurt or that we shouldn't feel the pain of it. No, they do hurt, and grief is necessary at times. But when we invite our Father of love into our grief, He will comfort and strengthen us, and He will renew our minds to see above the pain and to find the purpose we need to keep walking forward and trusting Him. He promises us, *"Never will*

I leave you; never will I forsake you" (Heb. 13:5). Like David, we can know, *"Even though I walk through the darkest valley, I will fear no evil, for you are with me; your rod and your staff, they comfort me"* (Ps. 23:4). He is the great and good shepherd of our souls. He is always with us, and because of His great love for us, we can truly say with Paul, *"I have learned to be content whatever the circumstances"* (Phil. 4:11).

Because I am an introvert, I have spent a lot of time alone. In the early years, at times, my introverted personality would cause me to feel lonely, but God groomed me through those lonely times. I could have become bitter or introspective. I could have accused God or others for the loneliness I felt. But instead, I pushed into more of God and His love for me, and as I spent time with Him, He changed my mind and taught me to be content in Him. I am content in knowing Him, in being filled with the power of His resurrection! I am content in the reality that I am not just legally one with Him, but that He is always *with* me!

When my children left for college, I again experienced a season of loneliness I needed God to meet me in. Having the twins move out at the same time was a big transition for me. I felt concerned that they would be happy at their new school, make the right choices, find new friends, and handle being apart from the secure nest of our home life. As a stay-at-home mom, my days and nights had been filled with caring for my kids for eighteen years. They were my full-time job, and I had truly loved that season of raising my children. Then suddenly, I had to adjust to less cleaning, less cooking, and a much quieter home life. Because my husband works outside the home, his life remained in many ways the same, but my whole world was shaken by their exit.

Like many women in this stage of life, I needed to rediscover myself apart from my identity as a mom. Through this process, as my husband and I both adjusted to our new identity as empty-nesters, we eventually stopped missing them so much and began enjoying this new season of marriage and my new role in ministry. As a family, we have always been very close, and I feel truly blessed to be a mom embarking on the new adventure of parenting adult children. I love watching them grow their own wings and fly into this world, knowing they will always be close to my heart.

And when at times I miss them, I am comforted by the Lord's presence with me. Even when I feel lonely for my kids, I am never alone. In every difficult moment, He is with me, and I can cling to His promise, *"My eyes will be open and my ears attentive to the prayers offered in this place* [to everything my daughter says]" (2 Chron. 7:15). I know He is listening to me and He loves me, no matter what happens around me, because He has renewed my mind to see the truth that surpasses all circumstances.

One time He made this so clear to me. I was standing in the shower, crying because someone had hurt me. And I heard God say, "I am close to the broken hearted." It completely changed my perspective. It didn't take away the pain, but it showed me the goodness of God in the midst of it. Suddenly I realized the person who had hurt me had actually done me a favor! Because when I'm broken in heart, God is close to me. Because of what that person did, I received a greater experience of God's grace and love and mercy, rushing in upon me and touching my heart in a deep way.

This is what the psalmist meant when he wrote, *"When my father and mother forsake me, then the Lord will take care of me"* (Ps. 27:10). When we are hurt and rejected by those who should love us, God holds us dear to Him, and we actually have a special place in His heart. He steps into our lives in a special way as Father, provider, husband, friend—soothing whatever wound has been created by the people who hurt us. It's all about perspective.

The apostle Peter wrote this encouragement to the early Christians, who faced awful persecution for their faith:

> *Beloved, do not think it strange concerning the fiery trial which is to try you, as though some strange thing happened to you; but rejoice to the extent that you partake of Christ's sufferings, that when His glory is revealed, you may also be glad with exceeding joy* (1 Peter 4:12–13).

In other words, he was telling them to renew their minds to see the good God would bring out of their suffering. We have a tendency to focus on ourselves and our own difficulty, but if we allow God to lift our eyes higher, we will experience His love and His goodness even in the midst of fiery trials, and we will watch Him turn our hard times into a testimony of His goodness. He did not orchestrate our struggles, but He will orchestrate our victory. He will use what the enemy intended for our harm to shape us into the people He's created us to be.

And when we come out of those difficult seasons full of faith and confidence in Him, He applauds us and says, "Well done, good and faithful servant!" Even though it is only His strength that gets us through and renews our minds to see above the struggle, He credits the success to our account. He rewards us for being faithful, for continuing to trust and love Him in the midst of difficulty. And He promotes us for being faithful.

CHAPTER 8

How Joseph Found
His Heart

Dick Mills prophesied I would be like Joseph—I would be betrayed by those close to me, and then I would need to forgive them. And he was absolutely right. Shortly after I came home from my visit to TBN, a new teaching began to circulate about "false brethren" creeping into the Church unaware. One minister began to accuse me and several others of being these so-called false brethren. At the time, my main messages were the believers' ministry, evangelism, and intercessory prayer—hardly anything false or dangerous. Suddenly, I went from being busy traveling three weeks in a month to having engagements cancelled because of these rumors against me.

Some of my friends didn't know what to believe, and instead of coming to my defense, they remained neutral in fear they too would be labeled false brethren. In the face of betrayal, like

Joseph, I had to choose to forgive and to trust God with the outcome in my reputation and ministry.

Years later, the minister who spread these accusations against me had a terrible shipwreck in life and ministry that took many years to rebuild. One day, in the midst of this process, she called me needing money and prayer for her health and her family. Because I had forgiven her, I was able to love her and pray for her without any bitterness in my heart. Thankfully, now this minister has been completely restored personally and in ministry. The other couple who had also been involved in the accusations against me experienced the same loss in ministry. Later, they came to me and apologized for all the hurt they had caused. To this day, we remain friends.

Forgiveness was how Joseph found his heart and became a great man who could save a nation. It is how we will find our hearts, too. Forgiveness is a big part of Christian maturity. It is what Jesus did, and it's what He calls us to do, but the only way we can is through encountering and being transformed by His *agapē* love. Only *agapē* is strong enough to forgive. Without it, we are helpless to truly forgive those who hurt and betray us. With it, we are empowered to live and love like Jesus did, who cried out, *"Father, forgive them, for they do not know what they are doing"* (Luke 23:34), while those who were crucifying Him gambled over His clothing.

For many of us, the idea of forgiveness may seem abhorrent or impossible. We have been so deeply hurt by others that we cannot understand the *why* or the *how* of God's command to forgive: *"Bear with each other and forgive one another if any of you has a grievance against someone. Forgive as the Lord forgave you"* (Col. 3:13). We need our minds to be renewed to see ourselves and others clearly and to understand the implications of God's forgiveness for our own sins. In order to forgive others, we need our minds renewed with some of God's truth about forgiveness.

1. It is OK to acknowledge the hurt and injustice of what others have done to us.

We see this in the story of Joseph. His brothers had sold him into slavery in Egypt, and for years he was a slave and then a wrongly accused prisoner in an Egyptian jail. In the midst of these terrible and unjust circumstances, Joseph learned to forgive. God softened his heart and transformed his mind to see His goodness despite his circumstances. This allowed Joseph to be the man God needed him to be in order to rise to power in Egypt and save that nation and many others from starvation during a great famine.

Then, because of the famine, his brothers showed up asking to buy food. At first they didn't recognize who he was, and Joseph had to wrestle in his own heart to choose to act out his forgiveness toward his brothers in a tangible way. We know this wasn't an easy decision because Joseph wept uncontrollably when he saw his youngest brother, the only one not involved in the plot against him (see Gen. 43:30). He grieved over the lost years with his family and still felt the pain of what his older brothers had done to him. When Joseph finally revealed his identity to his brothers, *"he wept so loudly that the Egyptians heard him, and Pharaoh's household heard about it"* (Gen. 45:2).

It was the moment of justice, and Joseph held all the power, but instead of using his power to punish his brothers, he wept over their reunion—probably tears of grief as well as joy. At first, his brothers responded in fear. They expected his full vengeance upon them. Instead, Joseph called them close to him and said:

I am your brother Joseph, the one you sold into Egypt! And now, do not be distressed and do not be angry with yourselves for selling me here, because it was to save lives that God sent me ahead of you. For two years now there has been famine in the land, and for the next five years there will be no plowing and reaping. But God sent me ahead of you to preserve for you a remnant on earth and to save your lives by a great deliverance (Genesis 45:4–7).

Then, weeping, he embraced and kissed them all. Here we see that even in his forgiving, Joseph did not cover over or diminish the wrong done to him. But he did release his brothers from the guilt of what they had done to him. When he forgave them, he told them they no longer needed to be angry with themselves for the sin they had committed. This is a powerful picture of what forgiveness can do.

But in order to forgive, the first step is to acknowledge the pain and injustice of what happened. Our hearts will not be able to fully release what happened if we don't acknowledge the pain of it and allow ourselves to grieve. Joseph genuinely suffered in slavery, imprisonment, and the loss of his family, and he wept loudly over that loss. That was the first step toward forgiveness. This is so important because seeing God's goodness in the midst of betrayal from others does not diminish the reality of what we lost or the pain we felt. God is the one who mourns with and comforts the brokenhearted (see Matt. 5:4) and commands His followers to do the same (see Rom. 12:15). He does not expect us to gloss over the pain of what we've experienced. Instead, He offers us a love that will truly heal our wounds, not just bandage them.

To those who are still carrying around the wounds of past betrayal, God is saying "What that person did to you was wrong. I see it and acknowledge it. I weep with you, and I validate your pain." Acknowledging the injustice of what we have been through and admitting how much it hurt us is the foundation to true forgiveness. When we do this, we bring it all out into the open and can give it to our Father. Then He can heal our hearts and renew our minds to be able to forgive. But if we hide or rationalize our pain, we actually refuse to give God access to it. If we won't give our hurt to Him, He can't heal it, and it will stay with us as a cancer in our hearts. So we must acknowledge the sin and how it hurt us, and then we must give it to God.

2. Our ability to forgive is not dependant on the other person's repentance.

Once we do that, we need to accept the fact that our forgiveness of a person is not dependant on that person's repentance. So often I hear people say, "All I want is for so-and-so to say that what he did to me was wrong!" The hard truth is that people are often unwilling to admit their wrongs or apologize. In Joseph's story, his brothers did repent for what they'd done, but only after Joseph had already forgiven them in his heart. In fact, the Bible does not make any mention of the brothers repenting until after their father had died (see Gen. 50:17). Clearly, Joseph did not base his forgiveness upon whether or not his brothers repented.

We, too, need to be prepared for situations when people do not repent, and we must find the fulfillment of our need for validation in our heavenly Father. He knows exactly what happened, how wrong it was, and how deeply it hurt us. He understands it even better than we do. And He cares. One of the most healing things we can do is to ask God how He feels about what happened. The truth of His love for us and His grief over our pain brings such healing to our hearts. It will enable us to choose to forgive, even when the one who hurt us remains unrepentant or even antagonistic. This is exactly what Jesus did for us, and it is the standard the apostle Paul puts before us: *"Forgive as the Lord forgave you"* (Col. 3:13).

How did Jesus forgive us? Did He have qualifications we needed to fulfill before He would forgive? The answer is no. He forgave us out of the extravagant love in His heart. Through His death on the cross, He forgave us of our sins and redeemed us from death while we were still unrepentant and rebellious (see Rom. 5:8; Eph. 1:7). His forgiveness is not dependent upon our repentance. However, our ability to receive His forgiveness and redemption in our lives is dependent upon our repentance. He has already given us the gift; the question is, will we accept it? This is the kind of forgiveness God has for us, and it is how He calls us to forgive others. He calls us to act in an *agapē*-inspired forgiveness that springs up out of our own renewed hearts, not one that is earned through the repentance of those who hurt us. God's forgiveness is completely unreasonable, and ours should be, too.

3. Forgiveness does not mean we don't set up healthy boundaries.

Of course, forgiveness is not synonymous with trust. And when we forgive people, it doesn't mean our trust for them is automatically restored, because while forgiveness doesn't need to be earned, trust does. Joseph tested his brothers to see if their hearts had changed before he revealed himself to them, because he wanted to know if he could trust them. He knew, once they knew who he was, they would subject themselves to him and beg for mercy simply because of the position of power he held. He literally held their lives in his hands. Yet he wanted to know the truth of what was in their hearts, so he tested them through an elaborate set-up in which they faced a parallel opportunity to betray their youngest brother, Benjamin.

And through this test, they proved their hearts had changed. Here's how it happened. Joseph hid a "stolen" silver cup in Benjamin's sack, sent the guards to find it, accused him of stealing, and threw him in prison. He told the other brothers they were free to go, but they refused, saying they could not leave Benjamin as prisoner in Egypt. Instead, Joseph's brother Judah said, *"Now then, please let your servant remain here as my lord's slave in place of the boy, and let the boy return with his brothers"* (Gen. 44:33). Judah, the brother who years before had convinced the others to sell Joseph into slavery, now offered his own life as a ransom for Benjamin. Joseph was undone by the transformation in his brother, and he wept.

God's forgiveness is completely unreasonable, and ours should be, too.

This was when Joseph knew he could finally reveal himself to his brothers. He had already forgiven them, but he tested their character to see what kind of boundaries he needed to have with them. The amazing thing about Joseph is that through all those years of hardship he kept a tender heart through practicing forgiveness. Often, betrayal can harden our hearts, but God wants our hearts to be tender and loving. This is what Hosea meant when he told the Israelites to break up their unplowed ground (see Hos. 10:12). He was talking about their hardness of heart due to the difficulties of life. To do this, we need to set healthy boundaries and refuse to let people use or abuse us in any way.

The reality is, some people do have bad intentions, and others may unintentionally harm us because of their own personal unhealthiness. They are not trustworthy, and though we should always forgive, we also need to discern proper boundaries for our own good. The only responsibility we have toward toxic people is to love, forgive, and pray. As we do that, God will give us wisdom regarding what boundaries we need.

4. Forgiveness will set us free.

God is the greatest psychologist we will ever have. Only He is truly capable of healing our hearts and enabling us to forgive those who have hurt us. We know Joseph was a godly man, because the Bible says God was with him, was kind to him, granted him favor, and gave him success in whatever he did (see Gen. 39:2–6, 21–23). About him Pharaoh said, *"Can we find anyone like this man, one in whom is the spirit of God"* (Gen. 41:38). I believe Joseph's closeness to God enabled him to become a tenderhearted man who did not become bitter or angry at the wrongs others did to him, but who lived with forgiveness in his heart and trust in God.

In his example we see that we do not need to be defined by the pain or difficulty of our lives. When we choose to forgive as God forgave, our hearts can be free and we can live in joy, no matter our circumstances. And it was this very heart attitude that prepared Joseph to be the one who could successfully interpret Pharaoh's dream and save Egypt and the surrounding nations from starvation.

5. God is our defender and avenger.

When we release our hurt and anger to God and choose to forgive, we give God the opportunity to be our defender and avenger.

It is His job, and He will do it in the best way possible. Joseph certainly did this. When his brothers came to Egypt for food, Joseph had all the power. He had charge of the food they needed, and he was second-in-command of the nation. He could have had his revenge in any way he pleased, and no one would have questioned him. We see how sincerely he had forgiven them in the fact that revenge did not even come into play. He did not punish them at all, not even with guilt. Instead he told them to forgive themselves, and he found a place of abundance for them to live in Egypt. He showered them with blessings.

So often we don't want to forgive because we want revenge; we want to make the person who hurt us suffer in some way. And in this we show our lack of trust in God's ability to bring justice on our behalf. We don't want to do it His way; we want it our way, and we want it now. However, when we allow God to renew our minds about forgiveness, He enables us to freely release our need for justice and revenge to Him. As the apostle Paul wrote, *"Beloved, do not avenge yourselves, but rather give place to wrath; for it is written, 'Vengeance is Mine, I will repay,' says the Lord"* (Rom. 12:19).

Once, a prophet gave me this message from God: "I am about to slap your enemies, and it is going to sting them so severely they are going to back off and stop messing with your life because I am your Father, and you are my daughter." Here's the key to this prophecy—I am not the slapper. God is. As Psalm 72:4 promises, *"He will bring justice to the poor of the people; He will save the children of the needy, and will break in pieces the oppressor"* (NKJV). In His time and way, He will bring justice. We need to trust Him with that, because often it will not happen as soon as we want or in the way we want. That is because God longs for *all people* to come to repentance. He does not want any of His children to suffer the consequences of their sins. He wants them to repent and be forgiven so they can be transformed.

Understanding and accepting this is part of the mind-renewing process. Too often we want revenge while God works toward redemption. When we truly trust God to be our defender and avenger, we will not need to see tangible evidence of the pay-back in the other person's life. In fact, we will pray those who have hurt us will repent and *not* reap the fruit of their sinful actions. We will continue doing what God has called us to do and walk in love, trusting God to take care of our enemies. When we do this, we will know our minds have been renewed.

Of course, people are not our real enemies. As Paul says in Ephesians 6:12:

> *Our struggle is not against flesh and blood, but against the rulers, against the authorities, against the powers of this dark world and against the spiritual forces of evil in the heavenly realms.*

The devil is our ultimate enemy, and he loves to sneak into people's lives and use them to hurt others. When people yield to his influence in their lives, because of their own hurt and anger, he uses them to try to stop God's anointing and purpose in our lives. We can prevent this from happening by trusting God as our avenger. The devil has already been defeated, and we know God will eventually take full revenge on him. In the meantime, the greatest revenge we can bring to our enemy is to love and forgive those who hurt us and to pray for their salvation and healing.

When we are hurt, we always have a choice. We can choose whether we will be angry or forgiving. We can choose, like Joseph did, to walk in love. Or we can choose to listen to the lies of the enemy and become a partner in his attempts to destroy other people's lives. It's that simple. Our part is always to do what God has called us to do, to walk in love toward our enemies and to set our faces like flint. God will take care of the rest. It's not our job to slap those who have slapped us. That's why Jesus said, *"If anyone slaps you on the right cheek, turn to them the other cheek also"* (Matt. 5:39). God is the one who will vindicate. Our job is to allow Him to renew our minds and heal our hearts. Our job is to pursue our own inner restoration so we can continue on with the work God has given us. Our part is to always walk in our Father's love.

6. When we forgive, God will redeem the painful situation for good in our lives.

Best of all, when we allow God to renew our minds, not only does He enable us to forgive those who have hurt us, but He also enables us to see the good He is bringing out of the injustice done to us. As we talked about in the last chapter, when we trust God and keep our hearts tender, He always brings good, even out of the most terrible situations. Paul the apostle, who experienced great suffering in his life, wrote: *"And we know that in all things God works for the good of those who love him, who have been called according to his purpose"* (Rom. 8:28).

In Joseph's life, this was the ultimate reality that enabled him to fully embrace his brothers. He was so thankful for the good God had brought in his life through their betrayal that he could not hold what they had done against them:

> Joseph said to them, *"Don't be afraid. Am I in the place of God? You intended to harm me, but God intended it for*

good to accomplish what is now being done, the saving of many lives. So then, don't be afraid. I will provide for you and your children." And he reassured them and spoke kindly to them (Genesis 50:19–21).

When we truly believe God's promise to bring good in it all, we will be able to do what Paul did: *"In everything give thanks; for this is the will of God in Christ Jesus for you"* (1 Thess. 5:18). The benefit God brings will loom larger in our minds than the pain we suffered. He will renew our minds and enable us to rise above and forgive.

CHAPTER 9

When Silent Tears Dry

One of the hardest offenses to forgive is abuse from a parent during childhood—whether that abuse is physical, sexual, emotional, or through neglect. Unfortunately, the need to forgive parents and find healing from abuse is a hurdle many women face. According to national statistics, about one in ten children suffer from child maltreatment. About 80 percent of these children suffer this abuse from their own parents.[8] Not only does such abuse hurt children physically and emotionally, but it also hinders their ability to view their heavenly Father in a positive light.

A friend of mine grew up with a father who abused her and her mother and siblings emotionally and physically. He also abused her sexually. And through it all, he would tell her he loved her and that was why he was doing it. The wounds of such abuse were very, very deep, and for years my friend hated the words *"I love you,"* even after she was born again. If that was what love was, she didn't want anything to do with it. But by the grace of God, my friend has found healing from her childhood experience in the embrace of true love from her heavenly Father. Now, those words mean more to her than almost any others. She takes them seriously, because she has experienced the absolute lack of love, as well as the engulfing and consuming *agapē* love of Father God. This healing, which is available to all, starts with the revelation of God the Father's consuming love.

Because of the large number of women who have experienced abuse or neglect from their parents and the effect that has upon their ability to know the Father, in this chapter we're going to renew our understanding of who the Father is. We've already talked about His radical love for us, but here we will specifically look at what it means that He is our *Father* and not just our God or Savior or Lord. This is so important for us to understand.

> *Fatherlessness is an epidemic in our nation.*

We all need to know Him as our Father, whether we've experienced abuse or not. The fact is, fatherlessness is an epidemic in our nation, and alongside those who were abused by their fathers stand many others who had absent fathers.

The enemy is doing all he can to handicap our ability to view our Father clearly. He wants us to cringe or shut down or become angry when we hear the word *father*, but God wants to renew our minds so we can really see Him for who He is. He wants to so woo our hearts that *father* becomes the sweetest and most comforting word in our vocabulary. He wants us to associate all kinds of warm and wonderful feelings with His name, *Abba Father*.

A *father* is a male parent—the founder of a race, a family, or a line. The word can also refer to any man who exercises parental care over another or to a person who has originated or established something. In these definitions, we see two basics of fatherhood—origin and care. A father is not only the origin of his offspring, but he is the one who takes care of them. Simply put, that is what a father should be. And that is exactly who God, the ultimate Father, is.

In the Old Testament, God was not known as *Father*. Instead, the Israelites had various names for Him, the most common of which was Yahweh (or Jehovah). Written Hebrew does not have vowels, so they spelled God's name YHWH. However, they referred to Him as Hashem (meaning "The Name") because they believed YHWH too holy to vocalize. Due to the lack of vowels in the Hebrew language, modern scholars are not certain of the exact pronunciation of YHWH, which is why some use Yahweh and others Jehovah. Other names for God included Jehovah Jirah (The Lord Will Provide); Jehovah Nissi (The Lord My Banner); El Shaddai (Lord God Almighty); Jehovah Rapha (The Lord That Heals); Jehovah Sabaoth (The Lord of Hosts); Elohim (God); Adonai (Lord); El Olam (The Everlasting God); and El Elyon (The Most High God).[9] These names highlight God's role as Lord of all, as well as some of the works He did for His people—like providing and healing. But none of them indicates a familial relationship.

Not until Jesus, the Son of God, came to earth was God called Father. The revelation of God as Father was hidden in these names, but it was not understood until Jesus came to reveal the Father to the world. John's gospel introduced Jesus in this way: *"No one has ever seen God, but the one and only Son, who is himself God and is in closest relationship with the Father, has made him known"* (John

1:18). Here, the word translated as "seen" (*horao*) means seeing with the eyes as well as with the mind. It indicates full comprehension, understanding, or experience. Prior to Jesus, no one had ever had a full comprehension, understanding, or experience of God. But now, Jesus has *"made him known."* This phrase comes from the word *exegeomai*, which means "to unfold or declare."[10]

And about His role as the revealer of the Father, Jesus said:

> *All things have been committed to me by my Father. No one knows the Son except the Father, and no one knows the Father except the Son and those to whom the Son chooses to reveal him* (Matthew 11:27).

This was the main thrust of His purpose on earth—revealing the heart of the Father in order to draw His lost children back home. This is why, even from a young age, Jesus continually referred to God as His Father (see Luke 2:49). But this filial relationship is not reserved only for Him, as the one and only Son of God. It is for us all. Jesus came to announce the invitation to join His family. Through His sacrifice on the cross, we all are adopted into the family as sons and daughters of God (see Gal. 3:26; 4:6; Rom. 8:17).

> *Yet to all who did receive him, to those who believed in his name, he gave the right to become children of God—children born not of natural descent, nor of human decision or a husband's will, but born of God* (John 1:12–13).

The bottom line of the whole story of human history is God's desire for a family. It was His purpose for creating Adam and Eve, and it has been His desire ever since. Thus, the parable of the lost son portrays God as an extravagantly loving father welcoming home His straying son (see Luke 15:11–32). And when Jesus taught the disciples to pray, He told them to pray to their Father instead of a distant Lord (see Luke 11:1–2).

In everything He said, Jesus revealed the Father. But He didn't stop there. The Bible tells us Jesus was an actual manifestation of the nature and character of God:

> *The Son is the radiance of God's glory and the **exact representation of his being**, sustaining all things by his powerful word. After he had provided purification for sins, he sat down at the right hand of the Majesty in heaven (Hebrews 1:3).*

In everything He did and said, Jesus was a perfect picture of the Father. This was a big change from the former way of thinking, as we see in Philip's question to Jesus.

> *Philip said, "Lord, show us the Father and that will be enough for us." Jesus answered: "Don't you know me, Philip, even after I have been among you such a long time? Anyone who has seen me has seen the Father. How can you say, 'Show us the Father'? Don't you believe that I am in the Father, and that the Father is in me?... (John 14:8–10).*

In other words, Jesus was and is the will of God in action, the character and heart of God made flesh. However, many people cannot see Him for who He is because the enemy has blinded their eyes. *"The god of this age has blinded the minds of unbelievers, so that they cannot see the light of the gospel that displays the glory of Christ, who is the image of God"* (2 Cor. 4:4).

When we see Christ clearly, we will see God as our Father, because He is the image of God and the exact representation of the Father. Through Him, we know what our Father is like. Through Him, we discover we are daughters of the best Father in the world, a Father who will never let us down or hurt us. And when our human parents fail us, He is there to pick us up, just like David said: *"When my father and my mother forsake me, Then the Lord will take care of me"* (Ps. 27:10 NKJV). In the Message version, this verse reads: *"My father and mother walked out and left me, but God took me in"* (Ps. 27:10 MSG).

He is the perfect Father, and in every area where our earthly parents have failed us, He has proven Himself faithful.

CHAPTER 10

Faithful Father

God is our perfect Father, the one who will never let us down. When our earthly parents are imperfect, He steps in as the Father to the orphan, and He heals our broken hearts and fathers us into freedom. Here, let's look at just a few of God's characteristics as our heavenly Abba Father:

1. Our Father saved us.

When the Father sent Jesus to die on the cross and redeem us from death into life, He committed the ultimate expression of love for us (see John 3:16; Rom. 10:9–10; 2 Cor. 5:17–21). As we talked about previously, Jesus did not give Himself for us to shield us from the Father's wrath (as some wrongly think), but He lived out the desire of the Father's heart for us. Only the Father could bring us back into His family, and that is exactly what He did. As First John 3:1 says, *"See what great love the Father has lavished on us, that we should be called children of God! And that is what we are!"*

2. Our Father provides for us.

Being the provider is part of God's nature as a Father (see Luke 11:13), and He continually provides for the earth and all who live on it, even when people do not recognize it. As James said, *"Every good and perfect gift is from above, coming down from the Father of the heavenly lights, who does not change like shifting shadows"* (James 1:17). When Adam and Eve turned away from Him, God immediately provided them with clothing to help them not feel ashamed. *"The Lord God made garments of skin for Adam and his wife and clothed them"* (Gen. 3:21). And that is what He has been doing ever since, as the psalmist attests: *"I was young and now I am old, yet I have never seen the righteous forsaken or their children begging bread"* (Ps. 37:25).

Jesus more fully revealed this side of the Father in His sermon on the mount, in which He talked about the futility of worry in light of the Father's provision. Considering the way the Father clothes and feeds the flowers and the birds, who are less valuable than we are, we can be confident He will also provide for our needs (see Matt. 6:25–34). *"But seek first his kingdom and his righteousness, and all these things will be given to you as well"* (Matt. 6:33).

3. Our Father heals us.

Healing is one aspect of Father God's provision in our lives that is mentioned many times in Scripture. Psalm 103:3 declares God "heals all your diseases." And this is one of the ways Jesus manifested the Father's heart on earth—by healing all who came to Him: *"He went around doing good and healing all who were under the power of the devil, because God was with him"* (Acts 10:38). This healing includes physical, emotional, and mental healing—and it is still available for us today. Our Father in Heaven does not change (see Heb. 13:8), and He still loves to heal the broken bodies and wounded hearts of His children.

4. Our Father is always home.

In the United States, about 1.6 million children between the ages of five and fourteen come home from school to an empty house.[11] But when we come home to our heavenly Father, we are not coming home to an empty house. As the story of the lost son shows, our Father is at home, eagerly awaiting our arrival. He can't wait for us to come home, and when He sees us coming, He runs to meet us and embraces us (see Luke 15:11–24).

Likewise, Jesus promises that His Father will never kick out those who come to Him: *"...whoever comes to me I will never drive away"* (John 6:37). Our Father is always available to us. He is never away or too busy. Instead, we are His priority, and He eagerly waits for us to come to Him.

5. Our Father listens attentively to all our needs, hopes, and desires.

Many fathers neglect their children simply through failing to truly listen to them and care about their lives. I experienced this in my own life growing up with an emotionally distant father. But the good news is our Father in Heaven longs to hear the secrets of our hearts. Consider this: Because He is all-knowing, He already knows everything that is going on with us, yet He invites us to share our hearts with Him because He wants relationship with us. He doesn't just want the facts; He wants the emotional connection that comes through heart-to-heart conversations.

In the Old Testament, when Solomon dedicated the newly built temple, God promised: *"Now my eyes will be open and my ears attentive to the prayers offered in this place"* (2 Chron. 7:14–15). Now we are the temple of God, and the Holy Spirit lives in our hearts (see 1 Cor. 6:19; 2 Cor. 6:16). Under the New Covenant, we have even greater access to Father God, and He listens closely when we talk to Him. Jesus knew His Father always heard Him (see John 11:41–42), and we can be confident He hears us, too. As the apostle Peter said, *"The eyes of the Lord are on the righteous and his ears are attentive to their prayer..."* (1 Pet. 3:12).

6. **Our Father loves us unconditionally for who we are, not for what we will become or who we think we need to be in order to be accepted by Him.**

Many of us had earthly fathers who became angry with us or emotionally withdrew from us when we didn't act in a certain way. As a result, we believed we needed to earn our fathers' approval. But that's not how our Father in Heaven works. As we mentioned before, He accepts and loves us unconditionally, just the way we are. *"God demonstrates his own love for us in this: While we were still sinners, Christ died for us"* (Rom. 5:8).

According to the apostle Paul, God caused us to be accepted apart from any of our own works:

> *Blessed be the God and Father of our Lord Jesus Christ, who has blessed us with every spiritual blessing in the heavenly places in Christ, just as He chose us in Him before the foundation of the world, that we should be holy and without blame before Him in love, having predestined us to adoption as sons by Jesus Christ to Himself, according to the good pleasure of His will, to the praise of the glory of His grace, by which* **He made us accepted in the Beloved** (Ephesians 1:3–6 NKJV).

The word translated here as "accepted" is the Greek word *chari-too*, which means "to make graceful, charming, lovely agreeable; to pursue with grace; and to honor with blessings."[12] Here we see that our acceptance is not based on anything we do but on His grace that pursues us and makes us beautiful. This is why Paul can boldly declare, *"Therefore, there is now no condemnation for those who are in Christ Jesus"* (Rom. 8:1). Since we are not accepted based on what we do, we cannot be condemned on that basis either. God is not like our earthly fathers. We do not have to measure up or walk some invisible tight rope of performance. He simply loves us for who we are, as we are, and no matter what we do, we cannot lose His love.

7. Our Father is not angry at us.

Many abusive fathers use anger to create fear and obedience and give themselves a sense of power. This is a very unloving environment to live in, causing children to feel constantly on edge and unsafe. Some people view God as being like this, but the Bible tells us another story. While we may assume He is thinking negative and critical thoughts about us, here is the truth: *"For I know the thoughts that I think toward you, says the Lord, thoughts of peace and not of evil, to give you a future and a hope"* (Jer. 29:11 NKJV).

In fact, the Bible makes it clear that fear, which results from anger, is actually driven out by God's love. Fear cannot stay when God comes; His love is that strong.

> *There is no fear in love. But perfect love drives out fear, because fear has to do with punishment. The one who fears is not made perfect in love. We love because he first loved us* (1 John 4:18–19).

Here we see that fear and love don't belong together because fear involves punishment. Those who grew up with angry parents understand this well. Angry parents are quick to punish because they are *not* acting in love. But as the love chapter reminds us, true love, God's *agapē* love, *"is not easily angered"* (1 Cor. 13:5).

8. Our Father forgives and forgets.

Not only is our Father not easily angered, but He also *"keeps no record of wrongs"* (1 Cor. 13:5). Unfortunately, some of us grew up with parents who continually brought up our past wrongs and held them against us. Such behavior is not loving. True love forgives offenses and never brings them up again. Psalm 103 describes God's attitude toward us and our offenses:

> As far as the east is from the west, so far has he removed our transgressions from us. As a father has compassion on his children, so the Lord has compassion on those who fear him; for he knows how we are formed, he remembers that we are dust (Psalm 103:12–14).

In other words, He has removed our past offenses so far away from us that we cannot even compute their distance from us. He does not hold our wrongs against us, but when we repent, He forgives us. Good fathers have compassion and mercy for their children because they know their children are not yet mature. Good parents do not expect their children to always get it right or act as a mature adult would. Instead, they love and accept their children in the midst of their immaturity and do not hold it against them. That is how our heavenly Father treats us.

Not only that, but His love actually changes us and enables us to grow up into greater maturity. *"If we confess our sins, he is faithful and just and will forgive us our sins and purify us from all unrighteousness"* (1 John 1:9). He doesn't hold our past against us, and He purifies us. He is such a good Father.

9. Our Father's council and advice are trustworthy.

Our Father is also the source of the best advice in the universe. We can trust what He says, even if it seems crazy. When we go to Him for wisdom and direction in our decision making, we will find our Father has unlimited knowledge of who we are and what would be best for us. He knows our hearts, and He loves our dreams. He gave us our gifts and our unique personalities, and He wants us to flourish in them. He knows what we are capable of, and He will not sell us short. He does not doubt our abilities, but He also knows what we need to be successful. He is the master of perfect timing.

We are blessed to be able to turn to our Father for wisdom, knowing He will not let us down. As James promised, *"If any of you lacks wisdom, you should ask God, who gives generously to all without finding fault, and it will be given to you"* (James 1:5).

10. Our Father is completely reliable, and He keeps His word.

When parents say one thing and do another, they create mistrust and a lack of confidence in their word. Children of parents like these often live with a great sense of disappointment and have difficulty trusting people's promises. This is a terrible environment for a child to grow up in, because a lack of trust creates a lack of emotional safety. Instead, children need to know the adults in their lives will keep their word, no matter what. And that is exactly what God the Father does. *"God is not human, that he should lie, not a human being, that he should change his mind. Does he speak and then not act? Does he promise and not fulfill?"* (Num. 23:19).

The answer is, of course, *no*. God does not lie to us, not ever. We see in Isaiah that God's promises are as sure and reliable as the properties and effects of rain water.

> *As the rain and the snow come down from heaven, and do not return to it without watering the earth and making it bud and flourish, so that it yields seed for the sower and bread for the eater, so is my word that goes out from my mouth: It will not return to me empty, but will accomplish what I desire and achieve the purpose for which I sent it* (Isaiah 55:10–11).

Rain does not fall to earth without watering the plants. It's just a fact of our ecosystem. In the same way, God does not speak without His promises coming to pass. In Jeremiah 1:12, we hear this promise from God: *"I am watching to see that my word is fulfilled."* He does not forget His promises to us. We can trust in the integrity of His words.

Jesus gave us an example of this when He trusted in His Father's promise to raise Him from the dead. What a risk the crucifixion would have been if Jesus was unsure whether the Father would keep His word. But Jesus was not unsure. He trusted unwavering-ly in God's promises, like this one from Psalm 16:

> *I keep my eyes always on the Lord. With him at my right hand, I will not be shaken. Therefore my heart is glad and my tongue rejoices; my body also will rest secure, **because you will not abandon me to the realm of the dead, nor will you let your faithful one see decay.** You make known to me the path of life;*

you will fill me with joy in your presence, with eternal pleasures
at your right hand (Psalm 16:8–11).

Here, God the Father declared He would not allow Jesus to stay dead but would raise Him back to life. After Jesus' resurrection, Peter quoted this promise in Psalm 16, saying it had been fulfilled in Jesus (see Acts 2:23–36). Truly, we have a Father whose word can be trusted.

In every way, He is a good and loving Father, and He wants to heal our hearts of the wounds caused by our imperfect earthly parents and transform our minds to see the great extent of His love for us. He is going to bind up our wounds, free our bruised hearts, and sew us back together again so perfectly that we will not have any scar tissue. At last, we will be whole by the presence and the power of Father God.

Paul described God's perfect Fatherhood in this way:

The Spirit you received does not make you slaves, so that you
live in fear again; rather, the Spirit you received brought about
your adoption to sonship. And by him we cry, "Abba, Father"
(Romans 8:15).

In Hebrew, *Abba* simply means "Daddy." It is the familiar term of endearment between a child and her daddy. God does not want us to live in fear of Him any longer. And He doesn't want us to refer to Him as an aloof and busy father either. He wants us to run to Him like a small child, to jump in His lap and call Him Daddy. Though He is the God of all the universe, we have a privileged place with Him and can freely and safely approach Him as His dearly loved daughters. He is the perfect Father (see Matt. 5:48).

A Love Like That

CHAPTER 11

When Broken Wings Fly

For a woman, two of the most significant relationships in her life are with men—her father and her husband. As a young girl, she learns about who she is and finds security in the love and protection of her father. When she grows into a woman, she leaves her father's protection for the love and protection of a husband who will cherish her for the rest of her life. At least, that's how it's supposed to be. But as too many of us know from personal experience, our fathers and husbands are not always what they should be. None of them are perfect, and some of them are downright mean. Some of them have clipped our wings and told us we can never fly.

In the last two chapters, we talked about how abusive and absent fathers distort our image of Father God, and we discussed what our perfect heavenly Father is actually like. In this chapter and the next, we will look at the equally prevalent and destructive issue of physically, verbally, and emotionally abusive husbands. Not only is God our Father, but the Bible depicts Him as our husband, too. We are married to Him, and He is a faithful Bridegroom. In other words, in every stage of our lives, He is the source of our identity and our personal health. He is the safe place, the one who praises and adores, the one who provides and protects.

Sadly, women who grow up with fathers who don't love and cherish them are prone to marrying men who won't either. This is another reason why encountering and being changed by God's love is so important. Only He has the power to restore our self-image and give us the confidence to make sure others treat us with respect. If we don't realize how important and valuable we are, we will allow others to abuse us—particularly our boyfriends and husbands. We may believe that's just how it is or we deserve to be treated that way. The truth is, when a man hits a woman, uses his words to shame her, or manipulates her emotions, he is disrespecting and violating God's daughter, and that is not OK.

God wants each one of us to know our worth to Him (which, as we talked about before, is not based on what we do but who we are). He wants us to really believe we're princesses, because when we do, we'll expect people to treat us like royalty. We'll expect our husbands to act like princes, to act like the greatest King of all—God. The Bible is full of imagery that describes our relationship with God as that of a husband and wife. On earth, marriage is the closest parallel to the spiritual intimacy we are designed to experience with our Creator. Thus, Isaiah wrote:

Do not be afraid; you will not be put to shame. Do not fear disgrace; you will not be humiliated. You will forget the shame of your youth and remember no more the reproach of your widowhood. For your Maker is your husband—the Lord Almighty is his name—the Holy One of Israel is your Redeemer; he is called the God of all the earth (Isaiah 54:4–5).

Here we see some important qualities in a husband modeled after God. He does not produce fear, shame, disgrace, or humiliation but instead enables his wife to forget the difficulties of the past and have hope for the future. This is what God does for us. He is not just our Father (our Maker), but He is also our husband, the one who redeems us from our past and empowers us to grow into maturity and beauty. He is the one, more than any other, who sees us for who we are and who we can be and who unflaggingly believes in us and calls us higher. This is the emotional and verbal climate a husband is responsible to create in his marriage.

The opposite of this is verbal and emotional abuse (or neglect). Physical abuse is loud and obvious, and we know it's wrong. But verbal and emotional abuse, though often more subtle, are just as damaging and just as opposed to the heart of God. We were made to fly, to be powerful and beautiful. But when we live in verbally and emotionally abusive relationships, the damage done to our hearts breaks our wings. This verse describes the impact of such abuse: *"A cheerful heart is good medicine, but a crushed spirit dries up the bones"* (Prov. 17:22). We are called to soar like great eagles, but we have been grounded and broken. We are stuck in our nest, missing out on the greatness of our destiny.

One of my dear friends—we'll call her Sarah—lives in an abusive marriage to a Christian husband. Over the course of twenty years, I watched as her husband's criticism, harsh words, and rejection chipped away at her, changing her from a confident young woman to one who is fearful, insecure, and full of self-doubt.

One afternoon I stopped by Sarah's house to pick up a pair of pants she had hemmed for me. I noticed she was dressed up and looking even more beautiful than usual, yet she was agitated and seemed fearful. Because I had known her a long time, I could see she wasn't herself. This wasn't the first time I'd seen her acting like this, and I had begun to realize it usually happened when her husband was around. When he was away on business, she was much more relaxed and an all around happier person. Our relationship had finally reached a place where I felt she might be receptive to what I had to say. And after many years, she was starting to come out of denial and realize how unhealthy her marriage was.

"Sarah, what is going on?" I asked.

"Oh," she said, pausing, "he is coming home tonight!"

"Why are you so anxious? What did you do today?"

"The laundry is completely done," she said, "and the house is perfect. I even lit a candle for atmosphere. I have been working out really hard to maintain my weight, and tonight I made his favorite meal."

"Well, then why are you so afraid and anxious?" I asked.

"Because I am afraid he will be angry," she said quietly.

"For what?" I asked. "You are an amazing woman, the house is perfectly clean, you look amazing, and most of all, you have such a beautiful heart!"

"Well," she said, hesitating, "I just keep hoping something will change—that he will see me for who I really am, the way my friends see me. I am such a good person. I do my best to make everything perfect for him, but he seems to always find something to criticize. Honestly, it's killing me inside."

And she was right. It was killing her—not physically but in her soul. She was quite literally losing herself under the weight of her husband's critical and destructive words. The Bible talks about this truth: *"The human spirit can endure in sickness, but a crushed spirit who can bear?"* (Prov. 18:14), and *"The soothing tongue is a tree of life, but a perverse tongue crushes the spirit"* (Prov. 15:4). Our souls are not designed to thrive without large amounts of love and encouragement. We need affirmation from the important people in our lives in order to become the women God made us to be.

At that moment, as I listened to my friend, the Lord gave me a prophetic Scripture for her from Proverbs.

> *A capable, intelligent, and virtuous woman—who is he who can find her? She is far more precious than jewels and her value is far above rubies or pearls. The heart of her husband trusts in her confidently and relies on and believes in her securely...* (Proverbs 31:10–11 AMP).

He told me to tell her these verses describe how He sees her and feels about her. "Tell her I am her Husband," He said, "and have her change the lower case *h* in the verse to a capital *H*. Tell her I am talking directly to her in these verses, and I want her to receive them like that."

So I told her. I read the verses to her and told her what God said. He is her true Husband, and He is rewriting her self-concept. He says she is capable, intelligent, and far more precious than jewels. To Him, her value far exceeds the value of rubies or pearls. He loves her, cares for her, and believes she is capable of fulfilling her destiny. He trusts her and believes in her. And my dear friend, as she heard God's word about her, received the truth of what He said about her. She took that truth and put it in the place the lies from her abusive partner once occupied. At last she saw that what her husband said about her was not a true reflection of who she was, and over the next months and years, her self-doubt lifted and her self-confidence returned. I watched her become like a beautiful, elegant, strong eagle—whose wings had been broken and then healed—take flight once again.

My friend experienced the truth of the promise, *"The Lord is close to the brokenhearted and saves those who are crushed in spirit"* (Ps. 34:18). Though her soul had been broken by the man who should have loved her more than any other, God still believes in and values her. And He stepped in to confront the lies she believed about herself. He changed her mind by telling her the truth, and that truth set her free (see John 8:32). No longer does she accept what her husband says about her. No longer does she allow his criticism and rejection to step on her heart and wound her spirit. She has found her strength and value in her greatest love, her heavenly Husband.

Because God has renewed her mind to see herself the way He sees her, she no longer lives under her earthly husband's cloak. When a woman is controlled or abused by a man, she wears the effect of that abuse like a cloak, and it affects everything she does. That shame and rejection from her husband actually becomes her covering and identity. We see this in God's rebuke to Israelite husbands who were being hateful and unfaithful to their wives. *"'The man who hates and divorces his wife,' says the Lord, the God of Israel, 'does violence to the one he should protect'"* (Mal. 2:16). The New King James translates this verse as, *"It covers one's garment with violence."* In other words, the cloak intended as a protection to one's wife instead becomes a cloak of violence and violation.

But when a woman renews her mind to understand who God says she is, she steps out from under that violent cloak and comes under God's cloak—the shelter of His wings (see Ps. 61:4). This is what my friend had to do. She decided to stay in the marriage, despite the abuse, in order to keep her family together, but she learned how to come out from under her husband's negativity and to rest in the shelter of God's approval. For her, this has involved seeing a therapist, reading books on the subject, and establishing healthy boundaries. She now recognizes that she is not the problem and that his words do not accurately reflect who she is. And she firmly and calmly stands up to him and tells him whenever his behavior is unacceptable. Over the course of several years, I have seen my friend become increasingly free from the effects of her husband's criticism.

At the same time, she has stopped trying to constantly please him through perfectionism, because this created a vicious cycle of sleeplessness and anxiety in her. Instead, she has built a life for herself with her friends and in doing what she enjoys. She wishes her marriage would change, but she has accepted that it may always be like it is. For this reason, she works on self-care and on helping others. She volunteers at a soup kitchen and does other acts of service that bring her joy. When she faces difficult times, she is able to turn to her friends for support.

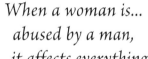

When a woman is... abused by a man, ...it affects everything she does.

My friend would be the first to admit her marriage is neither normal nor ideal. Yet through this process, she has grown much stronger internally. Her understanding of the truth of God's opinion about her (as well as the knowledge she has gained through counseling and books) has given her the power she needs to control her reactions to him; she is well-equipped to refuse to allow his words and actions to dictate how she feels. Her children, too, who are now well-educated adults, are able to see the dysfunction for what it is and understand it is not normal.

In this way, my friend has come out from under the negative effects of her husband's emotional abuse, and she has done all she can to protect the family unit and leave room for positive change and healing. No one's situation or solution will be exactly the same. The important part is learning to free oneself from the effect of the abuse—however that may look for a particular person.

When we come under the shelter of God's wings, His perfect *agapē* love casts out fear and builds faith and trust (see 1 John 4:18). This is God's ideal for all human relationships and especially marriage. This is how Jesus loved us, and it's how husbands are commanded to love their wives:

> *Husbands, love your wives, just as Christ loved the church and gave himself up for her to make her holy, cleansing her by the washing with water through the word, and to present her to himself as a radiant church, without stain or wrinkle or any other blemish, but holy and blameless. In this same way, husbands ought to love their wives as their own bodies. He who loves his wife loves himself. After all, no one ever hated their own body, but they feed and care for their body, just as Christ does the church (Ephesians 5:25–29).*

Husbands should love their wives sacrificially, just like Christ did. When they don't love this way, verbal and emotional abuse create fear, which brings with it torment, mistrust, and emotional walls. Thankfully, as my friend's story shows, women in verbally and emotionally abusive relationships do not need to stay under the abuse, even while they stay in the marriage. God always has a solution; He always offers hope. He wants all women to encounter His love and allow Him to renew their minds to see themselves as He sees them.

The first step is recognizing abuse. Sometimes our self-concept is so low we don't even recognize what is happening to us. Here are ten signs of an emotionally abusive relationship:

1. Critical and Negative Words

Words have the potential for significant damage. As the Bible says, *"The words of the reckless pierce like swords, but the tongue of the wise brings healing"* (Prov. 12:18), and, *"The tongue has the power of life and death, and those who love it will eat its fruit"* (Prov. 18:21). Words contain the potential for life or death. Words can pierce a woman's heart and paint pictures in her soul. Negative and critical words can create a long-lasting impression. When a wife is inundated with such words from her husband, her soul begins to wither and die. By contrast, the words God speaks minister grace to the hearers. Our words should do the same:

> *Do not let any unwholesome talk come out of your mouths, but only what is helpful for building others up according to their needs, that it may benefit those who listen* (Ephesians 4:29).

The New King James translates the last phrase of this, *"...that it may impart grace to the hearers."* Grace is "divine enablement"; it is God's strength in us that enables us to become the people He has created us to be. A husband's words should be this for his wife. When they are not, they create a deficit in her soul.

2. Neglect

Neglect manifests in a husband's lack of attention to his wife as a person and to her needs. Emotional neglect can look like the husband never making time to talk about things that are important to his wife.

3. The Silent Treatment

This is an act of manipulation, in which the husband tries to coerce the wife into submission by depriving her of his attention.

4. Indifference

Someone once said that the opposite of love is not wrath but indifference. It is the absolute lack of caring, and it is deeply damaging to a person's emotions. When a husband treats his wife with indifference, he communicates that she lacks all value.

5. Blocking and Diverting the Conversation

If a husband regularly changes the subject or finds ways to stop conversations in which his wife is trying to assert her opinion or needs, he is communicating a lack of value for her. Over time, this will bring a sense of futility and wear down the wife's desire to stand up for herself.

6. Ignoring

Like the silent treatment, a husband's decision to ignore his wife is based in manipulation and an attempt to degrade her self-esteem.

7. Belittling and Criticism of What the Wife Loves Most and Does Best

An abusive husband will usually attack anything that brings

value to his wife, especially the people and things she loves most and the abilities she excels at. He wants her to feel small and insignificant, so he regularly seeks to sabotage important relationships and may be emotionally abusive toward his wife's children and closest friends. He will also verbally attack or undermine his wife's attempts at doing what she loves. He hates anything that brings life to her, because it competes with him for control over her emotional life.

8. Control

A controlling husband punishes his wife verbally and through taking away or withholding things she values. Sadly, many men have used the Bible's teaching on submission to justify their controlling actions, but such arguments are completely false. Submission is something a person chooses to give; it is a heart attitude, and we are all commanded to submit to one another (see Eph. 5:21). Submission is a manifestation of love freely given, while control is a manifestation of selfishness forcefully imposed on others.

In the full context of Ephesians 5:20–32, we can see that godly submission has nothing to do with allowing a husband to abuse his wife or take away her self-control. This passage presents Jesus as the model for all husbands, and He is the Savior, not the bully or abuser. Properly understood, submission is a heart attitude that is not necessarily equated with obedience. We obey God, and we submit to one another. But we most certainly do not need to allow ourselves to be abused. Those who say as much completely misrepresent the heart of God. He has great value for each of His children, and He never forces us to obey Him or punishes us if we don't. As we talked about previously, His love is unconditional. He loves no matter what. And He hates it when His children abuse each other. The goal of a healthy husband-wife relationship is always to cherish and mutually submit to one another.[13]

9. Condemnation

The Bible clearly states, *"Therefore, there is now no condemnation for those who are in Christ Jesus"* (Rom. 8:1). A husband who treats his wife with condemnation, is unwilling to forgive, and continually brings up the past is not loving like Christ loves.

10. Devaluing of the Wife in a Variety of Ways

Ultimately, abuse arises from the desire to devalue the other. A husband is called to protect and honor his wife, not to bring her down and cause her to feel less valuable.

Each of these ten proofs of emotional abuse directly contradicts God's value for us and the way He gently and tenderly loves and leads us. He does not kick us while we're down or point out the ways we don't measure up to His perfection (though He truly is perfect). Instead, *"He heals the brokenhearted and binds up their wounds"* (Ps. 147:3). When our hearts are broken and bruised by the emotional abuse of the very ones who should have protected us, Jesus our Husband is here to bring healing. His words are medicine to our hearts: *"They* [God's words] *are life to those who find them and health to one's whole body"* (Prov. 4:22). His thoughts toward us are for good, not for evil (see Jer. 29:11).

Now that we've examined the symptoms of emotionally abusive relationships, in the next chapter we will explore how women in abusive relationships can take steps toward personal freedom and restoration of the relationship.

CHAPTER 12

Stand Up, Sister

God is the best Husband of all, and He longs to restore women who have suffered in abusive relationships by telling them what they're really worth to Him and showing them what real love looks like. This is what happens when He renews our minds. Suddenly we see that the abuse is wrong and the abuser has labeled us incorrectly. When we understand this, the next step is to start saying no to the abuse. Let's consider some respectful yet liberating ways to respond in an emotionally abusive relationship.[14]

1. Renewing Our Minds

As mentioned earlier, we must renew our minds to believe what God says about us. It can be difficult to shake off the lies when they were spoken by our husbands, but with God nothing is impossible (see Luke 1:37). We can do it! God knows us better than anyone. He has known us since before we were born (see Jer. 1:5), and He calls us lovely. The bottom line is, we must decide whether we will believe our heavenly Husband or our earthly husbands. Will we believe the words of the one who cuts us down or the one who lifts us up? Jesus is not like any other man in our lives. He is the perfect Husband and Friend, and He loves us at all times. Even the best and most wonderful husbands, like my own, will sometimes let us down, but Jesus will never fail us. When the apostles were threatened and told to stop proclaiming the truth about Jesus, they said, *"We must obey God rather than human beings"* (Acts 5:29). We must make the same brave choice.

One of the main ways we renew our minds is through reading God's Word. It tells us the truth about who we are and how God sees us. It is also powerful enough to bring change into our lives. When we meditate on the truth of God's Word, His Word actually begins to change us into the image of God. Paul said,

> But we all, with unveiled face, beholding as in a mirror the glory of the Lord, are being transformed into the same image from glory to glory, just as by the Spirit of the Lord (2 Corinthians 3:18 NKJV).

We behold the glory of the Lord in His Word. That is where we see Him, and that is where we are changed. Declaring what God's Word says about us out loud changes the way we think and helps us heal. Jesus used the Word to defeat the lies of the devil (see Luke 4), and we can, too. In Psalm 23, David describes how God our Husband comforts and guides us like a shepherd guides his sheep. Here is how the Amplified version puts it:

> The Lord is my Shepherd [to feed, guide, and shield me], I shall not lack. He makes me lie down in [fresh, tender] green

pastures; He leads me beside the still and restful waters. He refreshes and restores my life (my self); He leads me in the paths of righteousness [uprightness and right standing with Him—not for my earning it, but] for His name's sake (Psalm 23:1–3 AMP).

As we spend time with our gentle shepherd Husband, He leads us into places of internal rest and safety and restores our souls. As He does this, He also leads us into greater righteousness. What a beautiful gift from a perfect lover. Truly, He is consumed with love for us and longs for us to prosper and be healthy in all things (see 3 John 2). Just like I have a ring to signify my marriage to my earthly husband, I also have a ring setting me apart as the bride of Christ. This ring is a token of His love for me and a token of my love for Him. I take it seriously. I actually had a little wedding ceremony with Jesus, in which I pledged my faithfulness to Him. As we develop intimacy with Him, He will fill up the void created by what is lacking in our earthly relationships. He is our perfect and everlasting Husband.

2. Protecting Our Souls

As hard as it is, we don't have to allow abusive words and actions to penetrate our souls. Self-control is a fruit of the Spirit, and it means we have the power to make our own decisions and determine how we will respond to other people. This means we can establish emotional boundaries to protect ourselves from toxic and abusive people.

The Psalms frequently refer to God as our shield. *"But you, Lord, are a shield around me, my glory, the One who lifts my head high"* (Ps. 3:3). His love can shield our hearts from the arrows of abuse. If we try to shield ourselves from the attacks through denial, the burden of it will become increasingly heavy. As long as we hold the shield of denial, we are living in fear. Instead, when we use the shield of faith, we will be able to deflect all the arrows of abuse by embracing the truth of God's love.

God has not given us a spirit of fear but of *"power, love and self-discipline"* (2 Tim. 1:6). We are powerful women with God on our side, and we do not need to let the abusive words and actions wound us. Yes, it is hurtful when the men who should love us as Christ loves the Church instead treat us with rejection, criticism, negativity, and anger. But by the grace of God, there is a way to rise above it and to not take it personally. We are able to do this when we know the depth of God's love and look to Him to meet our needs. Also, recognizing that we are not the *real* reason for the unreasonable attacks will help us to protect our hearts. Abusers always act out of their own inner pain. Hurting people hurt people. When we can see them for the wounded individuals they are, we will be better able to remain emotionally distanced.

As we trust and lean on God as our Husband, He will perform a miracle in our hearts. He will heal our wounds and help us establish healthy boundaries. And He will harden us to difficulties. They will not be able to shake us and wound us like they have in the past because our hearts will be strengthened and secure in the love of our Husband.

3. Praying for Our Abusers

As God renews our minds and heals our hearts, He will also enable us to begin praying for our husbands. In order to sincerely pray for someone, we must first forgive (which we talked about in Chapter 8). Our prayers have the power to interfere with the work of the devil and open an avenue for God's love to break through.

What a powerful testimony it is to the love of God when wives are able to sincerely pray for their abusive husbands. God always desires restoration. The best case scenario is always for the abuser to stop abusing and to be set free by an encounter with God's love. We can't make that happen; we can't force someone to change, but we can make it much more likely through our prayers.

4. Confronting the Bully

Depending on the situation and the extent of the abuse, a wife may be able to confront her husband and tell him, "I am not going to let you do this to me anymore." As with any bully, there comes a time when forgiveness is no longer the issue. After every attempt is made to get along with a bully and that bully refuses to reciprocate and continues in his abuse, a Christian may rightfully stop turning the other cheek. In other words, if a bully does not stop his behavior after being told repeatedly to stop, the wife should pray about leaving the relationship. Often, a verbally abusive spouse's behavior becomes worse as the relationship continues, and if the wife stands up for herself, the husband may even become physically abusive. God's will is never for women to be battered, physically or emotionally.

I recognize this is a sensitive subject, and everyone's situation is different. Some women chose to leave these types of relationships, and others stay with the help of God and close female friends. My desire is not to say that one is the better choice but to point out the importance of not giving into a bully. In taking a stand, such a person is actually making peace by refusing to enable the bully to continue bullying. Obviously, the when and how of such confrontations vary according to the situation, and I always suggest first getting advice from a trusted counselor or spiritual leader.

5. Trusting God's Redemptive Power

As we talked about in the story of Joseph, our hope must rest in God's role as our defender and redeemer. What the enemy has meant for evil, God will turn around for our good (see Gen. 50:20). God didn't send the abuse or the neglect (see John 10:10), but when we keep our hearts fixed on Him, He will use it to make us stronger.

When we look to Him for wisdom and strength, trusting Him to defend and protect us, He will act on our behalf. It may not be exactly as we think it should be, but we can be certain that those who abuse us will not get away with it. God knows about all we've been through, and He will vindicate us. *"For God is not unjust to forget your work and labor of love which you have shown toward His name"* (Heb. 6:10 NKJV). He sees what goes on behind closed doors. Those who abuse us are touching the apple of His eye. It may look like He is not vindicating us, like He is ignoring us when we cry at night, but He is *not*. Instead, He is giving our abusers time to repent. He is wooing their hearts just as He has ours, because He is the God of love and mercy. He is the God of forgiveness and grace. And He wants to redeem abusive marriages into beautiful, healthy marriages that glorify Him. So He waits and woos, but He also acts and defends. He will not ever leave or forsake us but will rescue us and heal us. He will free us to fly.

CHAPTER 13

Let Me Be Your Mirror

When we encounter God's love and are changed in His presence, we realize outward circumstances no longer have to define us. We realize He is the most important person in our lives, and He becomes our mirror. What He says about us matters more than what anyone else has said. We realize we have the power to choose between God's voice and the voices of our fathers and husbands and other people in our lives. When we choose to believe Him above the others, what He says about us will transform how we see ourselves. He will be our mirror.

The Bible, which is God's love letter to us, says a lot about what God thinks of us. In this chapter, I will highlight a few of God's words to His daughters. If we really get this, it will change everything for us.

1. God says, "I know you."

To Jeremiah, God said, *"Before I formed you in the womb I knew* you, before you were born I set you apart; I appointed you as a prophet to the nations" (Jer. 1:5). Here we see that even before we were formed, God knew each one of us and set us apart for special plans. The psalmist echoes this idea when he writes:

> You have searched me, Lord, and you know me. You know when I sit and when I rise; you perceive my thoughts from afar. You discern my going out and my lying down; you are familiar with all my ways. Before a word is on my tongue you, Lord, know it completely (Psalm 139:1–4).

He knows us better than we know ourselves, and He sees all our intentions and the motives of our hearts. That's not something we need to be afraid of because He has made us beautiful: "I praise you because I am fearfully and wonderfully made; your works are wonderful, I know that full well" (Ps. 139:14). When God says, "I know you," it's not a threat. He's saying, "You are beautiful and incredible, and I know that because I know you and made you." We were formed in His heart before we ever took human form, and nothing can ever separate us from His consuming love for us (see Rom. 8:31–39). He knows us better than anyone, and He will never stop loving us. That means we don't need to hide from Him.

In God's words to Jeremiah we also see that being known by God includes being set apart for a purpose. We have all been ordained for a unique destiny on this earth, and He's given us the right personality and the best gifts to accomplish that destiny. That means, in order to be who we're made to be, we need to embrace the unique aspects of who we are. We need to love and enjoy our personalities and gifts, not sit around wishing we were like someone else.

We need to let that reality sink deeply into our hearts. He knows us and made us and loves us exactly how we are. He made us as we are because He has good thoughts toward us and is giving us a hope and a future (see Jer. 29:11). Thus, when He says He knows us, it means He knows what we're capable of; He knows we can do it! If we listen to other people's opinions, we will have a hard time doing anything, but when we look into His eyes, we will know we're capable of greatness. He made us for greatness, and He knows it's in us. He knows what we can handle, and He promises He will not give us more than we can bear (see 1 Cor. 10:13).

Gideon experienced this reality. He was hiding in fear, but God saw what was really in him. When God looked at Gideon, He didn't even acknowledge his weakness; He didn't acknowledge the fear. He bypassed it because He knew that wasn't really who Gideon was. It wasn't who God had made Him to be. Instead, God looked at Gideon's heart. *"The Lord does not look at the things people look at. People look at the outward appearance, but the Lord looks at the heart"* (1 Sam. 16:7). So when Gideon started complaining and talking fearfully, God spoke into his destiny by telling him he was a mighty man of valor (see Judg. 6:12).

He is saying the same thing to each of His children. He is calling us by our destiny, because He knows who we really are. People try to define us. They may yell at us, call us names, say mean things, or treat us wrongly, but we are not defined by their words. They don't know us the way the Lord does. He doesn't know us according to our sins but according to our destiny in Him.

2. God says, "I love you."

God's knowing of us includes His loving of us. The two cannot be separated. We've talked about God's love a great deal in this book, but we can never hear it enough. This is what He says about each one of us: *"I have loved you with an everlasting love; I have drawn you with unfailing kindness"* (Jer. 31:1).

3. God says, "I value you."

Not only does God know and love us, but He values us. He prizes us. We are the joy set before Jesus, for which He endured the cross (see Heb. 12:2). As He told His disciples:

> *Are not two sparrows sold for a penny? Yet not one of them will fall to the ground outside your Father's care. And even the very hairs of your head are all numbered. So don't be afraid; you are worth more than many sparrows* (Matthew 10:29–31).

The apostle Peter likewise said the inner, unfading beauty of our spirits as we respond to God in love is *"of great worth in God's sight"* (1 Pet. 3:4). We are worth the death of the one and only Son of God. He declares our great value to the world.

4. God says, "I accept you."

In Ephesians 1:6, God tells us He made us accepted in the Beloved (Jesus). In other words, we are accepted apart from what we do or how well we perform. We are simply accepted because of Jesus. This is a powerful truth that will set us free from the expectations we put on ourselves. One morning, as I was getting ready for my day and looking in the mirror, I heard God say to me, "You are accepted in the Beloved." It was like a boomerang in my spirit. *He accepts me! Even when my make-up isn't done and my hair is a mess, He accepts me!* Sometimes we spend so much effort making ourselves "acceptable" to others that we forget we are, at our core, already accepted by the one who matters most. In that moment, the Holy Spirit took that phrase, *made us accepted*, and downloaded it in my spirit. I realized that, unlike many of the people in our lives, God accepts us with His whole heart. Since the day we were born, He has chosen us as His bride and accepts and loves us unconditionally. His affection for us will never fade, disappear, or grow old.

5. God says, "I treasure you."

God values us, and He also treasures us. According to the *Merriam-Webster Dictionary*, the word *treasure* means "to hold or keep as precious, to cherish or prize."

When my daughter Jaclyn was little, she took ballet. As part of the class, she had to perform in a recital and be graded by the head ballerina. At the time, she was very shy, so performing like that was difficult for her, but she did it bravely. On the drive home, as I waited to turn at an intersection, I looked over at Jaclyn in her little pink tutu, her cute legs popping out beneath, and her hair up in a perfect bun. As she sat in the car, in all her adorableness, my heart turned within me, and I felt this burning love for her as my daughter. It's the kind of love only a parent can understand. I thought about how brave she'd been and how precious she is to me. All these thoughts and emotions were welling up in me regarding how much of a treasure she is in my life.

In response to these thoughts, I heard the Lord say to me, "And *you* are my treasured possession." I will never forget that day as long as I live. God was rewriting the script of my life, renewing my mind, and bringing me a greater confidence in His love. The love I had for my daughter in that moment exceeded anything I had ever felt, and I realized God feels the same way about me—

and all of us—all the time. When I went into prayer the next day, I looked in the Word of God and found where He declares to us, *"You will be my treasured possession. Although the whole earth is mine"* (Exod. 19:5 NKJV).

6. God says, "I honor you."

God also promises to honor us. The Hebrew word for "honor" is *kabed*, which means "to give weight to someone." It indicates importance, respect, consideration, and value. In the Hebrew mind, this metaphor for honor was connected to power and respect. It is like holding gold in my hand. I can feel the difference between 10 caret gold and 24 caret gold. Heavier is better. Thus, honor is the weight a person carries in one's estimation.

To those who love Him, God promises great honor. About such a one, God says, *"He will call on me, and I will answer him; I will be with him in trouble, I will deliver him and honor him"* (Ps. 91:15). In Isaiah, God promises to protect the Israelites for this reason: *"You are precious and honored in my sight, and because I love you"* (Isa. 43:4). He does the same for all His children. His honor for us isn't based on what function we perform in the Church but on who we are as His children and on our love for Him. Paul spelled out God's model for honor in the Church like this:

> *Those parts of the body that seem to be weaker are indispensable, and the parts that we think are less honorable we treat with special honor. And the parts that are unpresentable are treated with special modesty, while our presentable parts need no special treatment. But God has put the body together, giving greater honor to the parts that lacked it, so that there should be no division in the body,*

but that its parts should have equal concern for each other (1 Corinthians 12:22–25).

In other words, in the Kingdom, we all deserve honor, because God honors all of us. God doesn't operate according to levels of importance or significance. He gives the most honor to those who seem most feeble. God spoke to me about this once while I was making a pot on my pottery wheel. As I worked on this pot, it kept collapsing, no matter what I did. So I got out the blow dryer in an attempt to save it, and I dried the walls while holding them up with my fingers. When I was done, my fingerprints had dried into the walls of the pot. As I looked at my less-then-perfect pot, God told me to name it "Honor," and He said to me, "I honor you." That is how He sees each one of us.

7. God says, "I think about you all the time."

Many of us are well acquainted with the promise in Jeremiah 20:11: "'*For I know the plans I have for you,' declares the Lord, 'plans to prosper you and not to harm you, plans to give you hope and a future.'*" We need to let the truth of it sink into our hearts until we realize, as the psalmist did, how abundant and wonderful His thoughts are toward us.

> *How precious to me are your thoughts, God! How vast is the sum of them! Were I to count them, they would outnumber the grains of sand—when I awake, I am still with you* (Psalm 139:17–18).

Not once does He forget about us. Husbands and boyfriends may not always be thinking of us or considering our best, but God is always thinking about us for our good. The thoughts He thinks about us are good thoughts, good plans to create for us a peaceful future. He is the answer to the heart-cry for a husband to create a safe and happy home for us. Yes, we can experience that to a measure on earth through the love of godly husbands. But the fullness of the safe home is found in the heart of our heavenly Husband, who continually thinks good things about us and makes plans for a blessed and peaceful life.

8. God says, "I think you are marvelous."

When God created humanity, He declared us to be "very good" (Gen. 1:26–31). As the psalmist says, we are *"fearfully and wonderfully made"*—the marvelous work of His hands (Ps. 139:13–16). He made us marvelously, and He thinks good things about us (see Jer. 29:11). When we have negative thoughts about ourselves, those thoughts are not from Him but from the enemy. When those negative thoughts (which are really self-abuse) come up, we need to learn to say, "Stop it!" We should never accept those thoughts as truth. Instead, we should say, "Stop it!" and then begin to declare the truth of God's Word. "He thinks I am marvelous. I am wonderfully and beautifully made, and He loves me. He thinks only good toward me."

9. God says, "I am here for you always."

Like a good Father, God promises He will always be here for us. *"God has said, 'Never will I leave you; never will I forsake you'"* (Heb. 13:5). We do not need to fear abandonment; He will never forsake us. Even if we are forsaken by our earthly husbands, God promises to step in and fill the void.

For your Maker is your husband—the Lord Almighty is his name—the Holy One of Israel is your Redeemer; he is called the God of all the earth. The Lord will call you back as if you were a wife deserted and distressed in spirit—a wife who married young, only to be rejected," says your God (Isaiah 54:5–6).

He always comes through for us.

10. God says, "I forgive you."
When we repent, God forgives us. It's that simple. We don't have to cajole or beg for His forgiveness. Instead, because of His great love for us, He is eager to forgive us and move on. The psalmist says it this way:

As far as the east is from the west, so far has he removed our transgressions from us. As a father has compassion on his children, so the Lord has compassion on those who fear him; for he knows how we are formed, he remembers that we are dust (Psalm 103:12–14).

What a wonderful God He is—slow to anger and quick to forgive. We must listen for His voice. He is not condemning us but saying, "I forgive you. Accept it and move on. Don't grieve about what you did any longer. I forgive you." And we must forgive ourselves, too.

11. God says, "You are mine."
As the one who loves us more than any other, God says to each one of His children, "You are mine; you belong to Me." This dec-

laration is not possessive but protective. He doesn't say this to assert His control but to reassure us of His care and protection:

> ...Do not fear, for I have redeemed you; I have summoned you by name; you are mine. When you pass through the waters, I will be with you; and when you pass through the rivers, they will not sweep over you. When you walk through the fire, you will not be burned; the flames will not set you ablaze. For I am the Lord your God... (Isaiah 43:1–3).

With these words close to our hearts, we can rest in the truth—"I belong to my beloved, and his desire is for me" (Song of Sol. 7:10). No matter what is going on around us, the Lover of our souls is with us and caring for us.

What an incredible love God has for us! His words about us are so different from the words we often hear from others. They may even be different from our own estimation of us. But they are the truth. Let's soak in that truth until we really believe it:

> And so we know and rely on the love God has for us. God is love. Whoever lives in love lives in God, and God in them. This is how love is made complete among us so that we will have confidence on the day of judgment: In this world we are like Jesus. There is no fear in love. But perfect love drives out fear, because fear has to do with punishment. The one who fears is not made perfect in love (1 John 4:16–18).

As we agree with His declarations of love for us, we will be changed. We will learn how to abide in love, and we will be freed from fear. Anxiety will leave, and we will be empowered to respond properly in our relationships with others. The facts of our lives will change because we have been changed by His love. He will be our mirror, and we will discover how beautiful we really are.

PART 3

Continuing in His Love

*I*t's easy to feel passionate while attending a conference, watching a teaching video, or reading a book. The question is, how do you maintain that passion in everyday life? This book is about three steps to an intimate love relationship with God—experiencing His love, being transformed by His love, and then continuing in His love—learning to maintain that love relationship.

If you have the first two steps but neglect the third, you will lose much of what you initially gained. The good news is, the ability to maintain a vibrant love relationship with God is in your DNA. The end of this book does not mark the end of your encounter with God. Instead, it marks the advent of a new season of intimacy with God in your life.

Encountering God's love is only the beginning. As in any relationship, love develops through hard work and commitment. And the deeper love grows, the richer it becomes. Of course, God's love for us is already complete and full. He doesn't need to grow in love, because He is the fullness of love. He has known and loved us perfectly ever since He created us. We, however, need to grow in our ability to receive God's love and to intimately know Him and love Him back.

Love is an invitation, and it's our choice whether we stay on the fringes of the *agapē* party or move right into the center of the action. God will love us the same either way, but we will find greater joy and fulfillment the deeper we travel into His love. As the psalmist wrote, *"You make known to me the path of life; you will fill me with joy in your presence, with eternal pleasures at your right hand"* (Ps. 16:11). The great joy of knowing and loving God is offered to us in this life and for eternity. All we need to do is pursue Him, to give ourselves fully to building our relationship with Him.

In this final part of this book, we will examine what exactly it looks like to pursue an intimate relationship with God. In the first two chapters, we will look at mindsets that may block our intimacy with God. Then, in the next three chapters, we will discuss keys to a life of secret prayer and an inner life of communion with God. In the final chapter, we will look at a simple method of returning to Him when our hearts have strayed. These simple realities are the essence of a passionate relationship with God. Intimacy with Him is simpler than we may think. He stands with open arms, always, inviting us deeper into His embrace.

CHAPTER 14

The Way You Walk into the Room

The first step in maintaining a passionate relationship with God is having a correct perception of Him that enables us to enter His presence confidently. How we view ourselves and others makes all the difference in how we approach people. This manifests in two ways. First, we will expect others to view us in the way we view ourselves. If we view ourselves as unlovable, we will have a hard time believing people might like us or enjoying being with us. And if we expect others to dislike or reject us, we will approach them in a way that makes it easy for them to do just that. By contrast, if we approach others with confidence and generally expect people to like us and treat us well, most often they will.

Second, we will relate to others based on how we expect them to relate to us. If we believe others have a negative attitude toward us, we will expect them to treat us badly. And if we are fearful about how another person will act toward us, we will approach that person hesitantly, while keeping the exit in view. By contrast, if we feel safe in another person's presence, we will feel free to approach without fear of ramifications.

In both instances, we frame an encounter with another person based on our self-esteem and our perception of the other person.

> *If we feel safe in another person's presence, we will feel free to approach without fear of ramifications.*

In this way, our expectations determine what we will experience in our relationships with others. They are self-fulfilling prophecies. This can be either positive or negative. In both of these areas, we can be absolutely wrong in our perceptions, which results in unnecessary blockages to relationship. The question is, how do we know if the way we perceive ourselves and others is accurate? This is not always easy to discern, but it is crucial, and with the help of the Bible and the Holy Spirit, we can do it. And we must, because our ability to connect with others and especially with God is dependent on our perceptions of self and others.

Since the beginning of humanity, people have had a tendency to see themselves negatively and to expect God to do the same. But as we've already talked about in this book, He sees us through the eyes of *agapē* love. He is not the angry or stern or distant God so many of us grew up believing in. Instead, He invites us to approach Him without fear or shame, in the perfect freedom created by unconditional love.

To understand this, we need to look back to the Garden of Eden, where this wrong perception began. In the beginning, Adam and

Eve had perfect relationship with God. They were naked and unashamed. They had nothing to hide, because they felt completely loved and safe. Then the devil lied to them. He told them God didn't see them the way they thought He did. He questioned whether God was the good Father they thought He was. He told them God was trying to withhold good things from them, and they believed him. And their perception of God changed.

Adam and Eve chose to rebel against God by eating the forbidden fruit. As a result, they saw their own nakedness and, in shame, covered themselves. The fruit God had kept from them opened their eyes to self-loathing and insecurity. They had separated themselves from their Father, and for the first time, they were seeing themselves as rebels and orphans. The revelation was shameful, and their self-concept sank. They no longer saw themselves through their Father's eyes. They had believed a lie about God's intentions toward them, and they had seen their own sinfulness. Suddenly, their self-concept and their perception of God got in the way of relationship with God. They expected bad things from Him, so they hid when He came. They now believed they needed to hide and shield themselves from Him instead of running to Him with hearts of trust.

That is what happened when sin came into the world:

> Then the eyes of both of them were opened, and they knew that they were naked; and they sewed fig leaves together and made themselves coverings. And they heard the sound of the LORD God walking in the garden in the cool of the day, and Adam and his wife hid themselves from the presence of the LORD God among the trees of the garden. Then the LORD God called to Adam and said to him, "Where are you?" So he

said, "I heard Your voice in the garden, and I was afraid because I was naked; and I hid myself" (Genesis 3:7–10).

In Adam and Eve's response to God after the Fall, we see what the cycle of fear and shame looks like:
1. They covered themselves.
2. They hid themselves from the presence of God.
3. They were afraid of God.
4. They focused on their own nakedness and shame.

Many of us may recognize this cycle in our own lives, but the truth is, we never need to respond to God with fear or shame. He sees us exactly as we are, and He loves us. As we learned in the previous chapters, God's love for us is so good and strong that it can drive away all fear and shame. As First John 4:18 says, *"There is no fear in love. But perfect love drives out fear, because fear has to do with punishment. The one who fears is not made perfect in love."* In other words, if we are afraid of God, afraid He will get angry or punish us, we need a greater revelation of His perfect love. We need to change our self-concept and our God-concept to fit what He says is true. Then we will not respond like Adam and Eve but will run to our Father for help and healing and intimacy. We see this reality in Solomon's words: *"Though the righteous fall seven times, they rise again"* (Prov. 24:16). When we stay real with God and refuse to hide or cover ourselves, we will always find strength and freedom in His love.

These two simple guidelines show us how to properly approach God:

1. Approach God believing He is who He says He is.
In other words, approach Him with the correct perception of

Him. In Hebrews 6:11, it says, *"But without faith it is impossible to please Him, for he who comes to God **must believe that He is**, and that He is a rewarder of those who diligently seek Him."* In other words, we must approach Him with an accurate perception of who He is based on the Word of God. We must believe He exists and also that He is good and fair and rewards us well for seeking Him. We approach Him believing He is who He says He is. Our posture toward Him must be one of wholehearted trust, not distrust.

2. Approach God with a confidence rooted in an awareness of your own righteousness before Him.

Besides having a correct perception of God, we also need to have a correct perception of ourselves. God sees us as new creations. He has renamed us "the righteousness of God":

> *Therefore, if anyone is in Christ, the new creation has come: The old has gone, the new is here.... God made him who had no sin [Christ] to be sin for us, so that in him we might become the righteousness of God* (2 Corinthians 5:17, 21).

This is the truth of who we are in Jesus. We need to accept it and begin to see ourselves the way He does. Then we will be able to *"come boldly to the throne of grace, that we may obtain mercy and find grace to help in time of need"* (Heb. 4:16). We don't have to hide from Him. Instead, like the good Father He is, He longs for us to come boldly before Him as His daughters. He longs for us to feel so confident and secure in His love that we will approach Him with open hearts and truly believe in His love for us and His words about us.

CHAPTER 15

Fighting for the Glow

Once we have a correct perception of who God is and who we are in Him, we will be ready to enter His presence with confidence. The second step is recognizing the fight we're in. See, just like with Adam and Eve in the beginning, the enemy does not want us to have intimate relationship with God. Jesus explains this reality in His interpretation of the Parable of the Sower:

The farmer sows the word. Some people are like seed along the path, where the word is sown. As soon as they hear it, Satan comes and takes away the word that was sown in them. Others, like seed sown on rocky places, hear the word and at once receive it with joy. But since they have no root, they last only a short time. When trouble or persecution comes because of the word, they quickly fall away. Still others, like seed sown among thorns, hear the word; but the worries of this life, the deceitfulness of wealth and the desires for other things come in and choke the word, making it unfruitful. Others, like seed sown on good soil, hear the word, accept it, and produce a crop—some thirty, some sixty, some a hundred times what was sown (Mark 4:14–20).

In other words, when God's truth is sown into our hearts, Satan immediately attempts to steal that revelation and cause us to return to old ways of living and believing. He loves it when Christians are not experiencing the fullness of what Jesus died to give them. The enemy will do whatever he can to interfere. He will especially try to mess with our minds and convince us to believe lies about ourselves or about God, as we talked about in the last chapter. Recognizing these lies is one thing, but truly eradicating them from our belief system is another.

One of the most powerful and effective tools we have in the warfare over our mindsets and thought lives is our words. Science has confirmed what God told us long ago—that we actually create our beliefs through what we say and hear (see Prov. 18:21; Joel 3:10). With our words, we either agree with the enemy's lies or God's truth. Further, Hebrews tells us:

The word of God is alive and active. Sharper than any double-edged sword, it penetrates even to dividing soul and spirit, joints and marrow; it judges the thoughts and attitudes of the heart (Hebrews 4:12).

God's Word is living. That means His truth has the power to highlight and expunge the lies we have been believing. When we speak aloud the truth of God's Word, we are prophesying to ourselves, and we are literally changing the way we think. We are agreeing with faith and choosing to believe what God says rather than what the enemy says. For many of us, this goes against what we've done our whole lives. We've learned to agree with negative and fearful expectations about life. Without even realizing what we're doing, we may find ourselves saying things like, "Those mountain-top experiences never last," or "In a week, I won't remember anything I read." This is what the enemy wants us to believe. He wants us to think we can't maintain our zeal for God or truly apply the revelation we receive during spiritual experiences.

But that is not the truth. The truth is, we are made to experience ever-increasing glory (see 2 Cor. 3:18). God does not ever intend for us to plateau or to decline; His plans for us always involve an increase of His presence and goodness in our lives. Proverbs 4:18 describes this reality like this: *The path of the righteous is like the morning sun, shining ever brighter till the full light of day.* God's design for us does not include a sun set (not even in death) but a steady increase into greater brilliance in His glory.

Not only that, but the Bible tells us we have the mind of Christ (see 1 Cor. 2:16). That means, by the grace of God, we are not prone to forgetting what the Spirit has taught us. Instead, we are designed to be good learners who not only hear the Word but do it (see Luke 6:47–48). In fact, Jesus said the Holy Spirit would remind His disciples of all He had taught them and help them apply His truth to their lives (see John 14:6).

The apostle Paul talked about the reality of faith declarations pertaining to salvation:

> But what does it say? "The word is near you; it is in your mouth and in your heart," that is, the message concerning faith that we proclaim: If you declare with your mouth, "Jesus

is Lord," and believe in your heart that God raised him from the dead, you will be saved. For it is with your heart that you believe and are justified, and it is with your mouth that you profess your faith and are saved (Romans 10:8–10).

The truth is, declaring aloud our faith in God's Word and agreeing with its application in our lives is an essential part of Christian growth. As we declare our faith in Him, we experience change in our lives. As we declare the truth about who He is and how He sees us, we enter into deeper intimacy with Him. We simply need to put the Word of God in our hearts and speak it from our mouths. We need to meditate on the truth of God's Word written in this book and in the Bible. This is how we maintain the glow of love, the passion of relationship with God, in the midst of daily life.

When the enemy approaches, trying to get us to question the truth of God's love for us, we can stand strong and declare truth from God's Word, including:

I am fearfully and wonderfully made (see Ps. 139:14).

I am loved with an everlasting love (see Jer. 31:3).

I am accepted in the Beloved (see Eph. 1:6).

God will never leave me or forsake me (see Heb. 13:5).

I am confident and secure in His love (see Ps. 112:6).

I know who I am (see Song of Sol. 7:10).

The Word of God is the sword of the Spirit because it is a great defense and weapon against the enemy's lies (see Eph. 6:17). When we use this chief weapon of our warfare, we will *"be strong in the Lord and in his mighty power"* (Eph. 6:10). To start, declare aloud right now, "I am going to maintain my glow! I am not going to allow the devil to steal the Word from me!"

CHAPTER 16

Passion in the Prayer Closet

Now that we've addressed our mindsets, let's look at the first practical tool to growing in intimacy with God—secret prayer. We fan the fire of passion through secret prayer in our homes, cars, closets, or wherever we can find alone and undistracted time in His presence. In the place of secret prayer, we give God our full attention, with no distractions. If the New Agers can spend at least fifteen minutes a day in meditation, we, as born again children of God, should be able to do even more to cultivate our love relationship with Him. If we chose not to, our relationship with Him will weaken. If a husband and wife went six days out of every week without speaking, we would hardly say they had an intimate relationship. The same is true of our relationship with God.

If we want to be close to Him and keep the fire burning, we need to work at our relationship by spending time with Him one-on-one.

Corporate gatherings are good and necessary, but we must each have an individual relationship with God that is not fanned by the passion of those around us but by the passionate intimacy built through time alone with the one we love. Intimacy requires complete, wholehearted focus. We need to free ourselves from the manifold distractions of life and simply gaze into His eyes, like lovers do. This is why being alone with Him is so important. If He has to continually compete with the things of life for our attention, we will have a hard time really learning to know Him.

That is what secret prayer is all about. We see this in Jesus' relationship with His disciples while He lived on earth. He spoke many parables to the crowds, but He only explained them to His disciples when He was alone with them:

> *With many similar parables Jesus spoke the word to them, as much as they could understand. He did not say anything to them without using a parable. But when he was alone with his own disciples, he explained everything* (Mark 4:33–34).

In this we see the special connection that comes through spending time alone with God. Even Jesus had a private life of prayer while He lived on earth. Though He was fully God (while also being fully man), He too needed to practice secret prayer with His Father. The gospels tell us He at various times withdrew to *"a solitary place"* (Matt. 14:13; Mark 1:35; Luke 4:42). Once, after He had sent the multitudes away, He went up to a mountain by Himself to pray (Matt. 14:23). Luke 5:16 gives this simple commentary on Jesus' prayer life: *"Jesus often withdrew to lonely places and prayed."* Clearly, He loved spending time alone with His Father.

If Jesus needed secret prayer in His life, it's safe to say we need it, too. The question is, why? What is the purpose of secret prayer? What do we gain from spending time alone with Him? And the answer is simple. Secret prayer produces *intimacy*.

Webster's dictionary defines *intimacy* as "associated in close personal relations, involving warm friendship or a personally close or familiar association, private, or closely personal; an association, knowledge or understanding arising from close personal connection or familiar experience." That is the sort of relationship God invites us into. It's not just a side benefit but the core of our faith, which is not based on rules but on relationship.

We see this reality in Philippians 3:10, where the apostle Paul explains his purpose in life:

> [For my determined purpose is] that I may know Him [that I may progressively become more deeply and intimately acquainted with Him, perceiving and recognizing and understanding the wonders of His Person more strongly and more clearly]... (AMP).

Paul didn't find his purpose in planting churches throughout the world, being an apostle, or writing two thirds of the New Testament. Paul knew that no matter what he did, his purpose was always simply to know Jesus intimately. That should be our purpose, too. Without an intimate love relationship with God, nothing else we may do matters. And that is the foremost fruit of secret prayer.

Nothing compares to the experience of intimacy with God, the feeling of closeness with the King of all. Nothing compares to encountering Him one-on-one and realizing, *He showed up just for me!* He wants to visit each one of us; He loves to whisper His secrets to those who take the time to become His friends and listen to His heart. He is not withholding Himself or hiding from us; all we need to do is get alone with Him and invite Him to speak to our hearts.

Moses is another biblical example of someone who prized intimacy with God above all else. About him the Bible says, *"The Lord would speak to Moses face to face, as one speaks to a friend..."* (Exod. 33:11). This verse always reminds me of one of my favorite worship songs, "Show me Your face, Lord..."[15] We are able to ask to see His face because the spirit realm is actually more real than the natural. Though we usually can't see it with our eyes, the spiritual realm preceded the natural world, and as children of God, we are invited to see into that invisible spiritual realm. We are invited to seek God's face just like Moses did.

It's encouraging to know that Moses didn't always hunger for God's face. He didn't always experience that deep intimacy with Him. He was human just like us, and when he first encountered God, his response was much different:

> Then he said, "I am the God of your father, the God of Abraham, the God of Isaac and the God of Jacob." At this, Moses hid his face, because he was afraid to look at God (Exodus 3:6).

Moses hid his face from God because He was afraid to look at God. This is surprising considering what we know of Moses later in his life. Once I asked God, "What changed between Exodus 3 and Exodus 33?" He told me Moses had learned to know Him and understand Him. He had seen God's faithfulness and His love toward His people, and that changed everything. Moses learned to know God through faithfully spending time in His presence. And through that knowledge, he developed an intimacy between himself and God.

If it was possible for Moses, under the Old Covenant, it is even more possible for us. We, in the New Covenant, are able to have an even greater relationship than Moses did with our heavenly Father. That is my quest in life—to become deeply and intimately acquainted with God, to know the wonders of His person, to perceive and recognize who He is. As Andrew Murray said, "O let the place of secret prayer become to me the most beloved spot on earth."[16] We are all invited into this kind of intimacy with Him. All we need to do is seek His face.

Moses spent the latter part of his life seeking God's face, and as a result, this was his legacy:

> *Since then, no prophet has risen in Israel like Moses, whom the Lord knew face to face, who did all those signs and wonders the Lord sent him to do in Egypt—to Pharaoh and to all his officials and to his whole land. For no one has ever shown the mighty power or performed the awesome deeds that Moses did in the sight of all Israel* (Deuteronomy 34:10–12).

More than anything else, Moses was known as a man who knew God face-to-face. What a legacy! Yes, he performed signs and wonders, delivered the nation from Egypt, and led them across the wilderness to the Promised Land, but his foremost legacy was the depth of intimacy he had with God.

The story of Moses reminds me of a more recent hero in the faith—Kenneth E. Hagin, who valued intimacy with God above all else. I graduated from Rhema Bible Training College, which

Kenneth E. Hagin founded, and more than once I heard him say, "Jesus is more real to me than my wife next to me in the bed." What a profound and challenging idea. That kind of intimacy with God is possible for each one of us. One of the keys is the secret place and practice of prayer. In that place, we will be transformed. As someone once said: "In prayer we learn to change. Prayer is one of the most changing experiences we will ever know." As we behold God, we will become like Him (see 2 Cor. 3:18). And we will develop a deep and passionate intimacy with the lover of our souls.

CHAPTER 17

Burning Hearts

I first learned how to pray when I was at Rhema. Even though I was receiving incredible teaching there, I still felt dissatisfied. I wanted something more. It wasn't that I was bored. I was learning a lot and enjoyed it, yet my spirit knew there must be more. I felt a deep hunger for God. My heart burned for Him, and I knew He was drawing me away to be with Him. I knew I was His beloved and He was mine, and I found satisfaction by going into a literal closet in my apartment, shutting that door, and entering into that quiet place where I could seek the face of God. That closet was where I encountered God in the intimacy my heart burned for.

All of us, in our hearts, long for intimacy with God, and nothing can satisfy that longing but Him. Only in the secret place of prayer will we discover the heights and the depths of His love and learn to know Him intimately. This is why it is so important for us to develop the practice of secret prayer in our lives. Many people find the idea of prayer very intimidating, but it is actually simple. We were made to commune privately with our God, and we will find our greatest pleasure and fulfillment as we do. In this chapter, I will give a few pointers for how to develop a lifestyle of secret prayer.[17]

1. Dedicate a Place for Secret Prayer

The first step is simply to pick a place where you will spend your alone time with God, either at your home or at your office. In Matthew 6:6, Jesus introduced the idea of secret prayer to His disciples:

> But you, when you pray, go into your room, and when you have shut your door, pray to your Father who is in the secret place; and your Father who sees in secret will reward you openly (NKJV).

The word *closet* in this verse is translated from the Greek word *tameion*, which denotes any private room, secret chamber, or inner chamber. This is the place of privacy where you pray and are alone with God. As Leonard Ravenhill put it: "The secret of praying is praying in secret."[18] All we need to do is pick a place and get started. It could be simply a corner of the house or a seat by the window. It doesn't need to be fancy; it just needs to be a place we can dedicate to meeting with God. The reward for doing so will be great. Jesus made it clear that God openly rewards those who practice secret prayer. These rewards include greater anointing, a greater experience of His abiding presence, and the continual burning of our hearts with the fire of God's love.

2. Practice Visualization

Once we've found our secret place, the second step is to practice visualization. To some, this may sound like the New Age, but the truth is that visualization started with God, and the New Age copied it from Him. For example, consider Isaiah 26:3, which says, *"You will keep him in perfect peace, whose mind is stayed on [fixed on] You, because he trusts in You."* Our minds use images to process information. We cannot think about a pink horse without picturing a pink horse in our heads. Thus, it is very difficult for us to fix our minds on God without visualizing what the Word of God says about Him and our relationship with Him. This is what biblical meditation is all about (see Josh. 1:8).

In fact, the Bible tells us that visually meditating on the glory of God (His divine attributes and wonderful acts) will cause us to become like Him.

> *But we all, with unveiled face, beholding as in a mirror the glory of the Lord, are being **transformed** into the same image from glory to glory, just as by the Spirit of the Lord* (2 Corinthians 3:18).

When we look at Him, we become what we behold. This is the power of biblical visualization. Simply put, visualization means going into prayer remembering who He is and what He says about us. It means keeping before us the revelation of His character in the Word of God. That's how we know what God looks like. For example, the Bible tells us God is merciful. We can visualize this attribute of God by thinking about something merciful we have seen Him do in our lives. We can visualize Him by imagining His acts of love toward humanity. We can even behold His humor by imagining Jesus laughing and making jokes with His disciples and playing with the children. Because we know He says we are marvelous, we can imagine ourselves as princesses. We can imagine our Father the King looking at us with love in His eyes. These are just a few examples.

Whenever we want to visualize an aspect of God's character or the meaning of a truth from His Word, we can ask Holy Spirit to help us imagine what that truth looks like. "What does it look like, God, that You are the God of peace?" And He will give us images to help us comprehend more fully His unfathomable glory. We only really begin to understand what words mean when we experience them.

The definition of *love* isn't enough. We need to experience it to understand it. This is how we behold God, how we build intimacy with Him, and how we become more and more like Him.

Visualization also helps us maintain focus in prayer. We are easily distracted when we're trying to concentrate on abstract concepts. But our minds can be captivated by images. The Book of Revelation describes Jesus (see Rev. 1:9–20), and the Word of God contains many pictorial descriptions of God. Using these, we can imagine Him with us. On the screen saver of my phone, I have a visualization, a picture of Mary at the feet of Jesus. When I'm in the secret place of prayer and I find my mind wandering or I'm getting tired or my stomach's growling, I focus my attention on Jesus by using this picture. Sometimes I literally visualize Jesus standing before me, and I get down on my knees and start worshiping Him, or I talk to Him.

God made our minds the way they are for a reason. Our imag-

> *The definition of love isn't enough. We need to experience it.*

inations are not bad; they are a tool to help us engage the unseen realm. Using our minds to visualize the truths of the Bible will increase our intimacy with Jesus. And as we look into the face of Jesus and visualize His goodness, we will be transformed into His image!

3. Practice Silence

A third tool useful in the practice of secret prayer is silence. When we think of prayer, we don't usually think of silence, but the Bible actually mentions it several times. In the Psalms, we are told, "**Be still**, *and know that I am God*" (Ps. 46:10a), and "*...Meditate within your heart* **on your bed, and be still**" (Ps. 4:3 NKJV). Likewise, Jesus told His disciples, "*When you pray, do not keep on babbling like pagans, for they think they will be* **heard because of their many words**" (Matt. 6:7). Honestly, when it comes to prayer, I think much of the Church has completely missed it. We've been so busy in our praying when sometimes God wants us to simply stop talking and be still.

Don't get me wrong. It is OK to pray long-winded prayers and to talk to God a lot. He loves when we talk to Him, and prayer does open doors for God to work. However, silence is also important. I learned this in a very real way during a prayer event I led years ago. We were all dancing and singing and praying when I felt God speak to me so clearly, "My eyes are open, and My ears are attentive to the prayers being made in this place. I get it. And I want you to come up higher. I want you to all be still and know that I am God!"

The church hosting the event is an amazing church where people love God and love to pray, and that night people were worshipping God loudly and wholeheartedly. Hearing God's request, I looked around and wondered how I could make a transition like that happen. Fortunately, I didn't have to. As I sat there, suddenly a holy hush came into the building, and the presence of God was so thick that I don't think we could have said anything even if we had wanted to. Twenty minutes passed like that. No one said a word. No children cried. Everyone was still and silent. It was a powerful time.

There's a time to pray aloud and a time to be quiet. At times, we need to practice silence in prayer. We need to simply be with Him and know Him in quietness. God speaks in the silence. He restores and mends in the silence. We find divine rest in silence with God. In our private times of prayer, let's be sure to make time for silence.

4. Practice Inward Reflection

Inward reflection is the fourth important tool for building a strong prayer life in the secret place with God. While silence before God is a quiet listening and waiting, reflection is an active internal prayer and meditation on the attributes of God. It often involves silent worship from the heart, as well as a heart yearning and adoration that transcends words. It is the inward communion of our spirits with the Spirit of God.

The Result: Hearts that Burn

The combination of visualization, silence, and reflection in our secret place of prayer with God will produce an amazing intimacy. Our hearts will be so connected to His that we will recognize His presence even when we can't see Him. We will be able to quickly discern when He's near because our hearts will burn within us. We find this concept in the account of the two disciples who walked the seven miles from Jerusalem to Emmaus, discussing the events surrounding Jesus' death with Jesus Himself—

only they did not recognize Him. *"As they talked and discussed these things with each other, Jesus himself came up and walked along with them; but they were kept from recognizing him"* (Luke 24:15–16). Jesus drew near to them, but they failed to recognize Him. So He asked them about their conversation and then, *"beginning with Moses and all the Prophets, he explained to them what was said in all the Scriptures concerning himself"* (Luke 24:27).

At the end of seven miles, they arrived at Emmaus and invited Jesus to stay with them, though He would have gone farther. Jesus agreed to go with them, and as He sat down to eat with them, He took the bread, blessed and broke it, and gave it to them. Immediately, their eyes were opened to recognize Him, and He vanished from their sight. Reflecting on their experience, these disciples said to each other, *"Were not our hearts burning within us while he talked with us on the road and opened the Scriptures to us?"* (Luke 24:32).

Jesus, the very one they longed for, had risen from the dead and come near to them, but they did not recognize Him. It's somewhat mindboggling to consider the fact that these two had spent three years traveling with and listening to Jesus, yet they didn't recognize Him. Instead, they were stressed out and grieving because they thought their world had fallen apart. They didn't understand what it all meant. Jesus, ever compassionate, began to explain it all to them, helping them understand the plan of salvation and the purpose for His death. When they had received the truth from Him, they sat down to commune with Him over a meal, and that was when they recognized Him. Afterward, they realized their hearts had recognized Him all along. Their hearts had burned within them because of His presence with them.

They didn't recognize it immediately, but we can. That is the accumulated effect of secret prayer. It keeps the fire of our passion for Him burning. And when He draws near, our hearts begin to burn in His presence. When I sense Him drawing near, I get quiet and still and simply soak in His presence. I immerse myself fully in Him, and I allow Him to fan the flames of my heart. This is the beauty, the passion, the pleasure of cultivating intimacy with God in the place of secret prayer.

CHAPTER 18

The Inward Life

The second key to intimacy with God is similar to the first. Just like we need that hidden place of secret prayer, where we can enjoy one-on-one time with Jesus, we also need to maintain our inner life and dialogue with God throughout the day.[19] This doesn't happen in the prayer closet but in the secret place of our hearts. Simply defined, the inward life of prayer is an inner dialogue with God in the secret place of our hearts while we go about our daily activities. This practice will take us to deeper levels with Him. The world observes, to varying degrees, our outward lives, but only God sees our inward lives. This is what the apostle Paul referred to when he wrote, "...*Though outwardly we are wasting away, yet inwardly we are being renewed day by day*" (2 Cor. 4:16). The apostle Peter also compared the outward reality with the inward when he wrote:

> *Your beauty should not come from outward adorn-*
> *ment, such as elaborate hairstyles and the wear-*

ing of gold jewelry or fine clothes. Rather, it should be that of your inner self, the unfading beauty of a gentle and quiet spirit, which is of great worth in God's sight (1 Peter 3:3–4).

We renew and beautify our inner selves through that inner dialogue with God as we go about our daily activities. In the hidden place of our hearts, we are able to build a special and intimate relationship with Him.

Like God, we are tri-part beings. We are spirits who have souls and live in bodies. This means we have contact with three realms of reality—the spirit world, the intellectual world, and the physical world. Within ourselves, we communicate from each of these realms. So the voice of the spirit is our conscience, the voice of the soul is our reason, and the voice of the body is our feelings. This is important to understand so we can discern what voice we're listening to. When we are born again, our spirits are united with the Holy Spirit of God. He comes to live in us and walk with us (see Eph. 2:22). This means He is with us and in us at all times, and we can talk to Him at any time. We do not have to go to a special place, like the Temple, because we now are the temple: *"Don't you know that you yourselves are God's temple and that God's Spirit dwells in your midst?"* (1 Cor. 3:16).

Thus, in a very real way, we can walk through life with God, continually talking with Him about life just as we would a close friend. This is what it means to commune with God in our spirits. As we do this regularly, our perspective begins to shift, and our inner world of relationship with God becomes more real to us than our outer existence. Our insides become more real than our outsides. This may sound strange, but it is what happens when we become God-minded. Our focus shifts to the eternal and spiritual more than the temporal and physical realities of life on earth. This doesn't mean we don't care about the things of earth but that we see them from God's perspective. This is what it means to live a life of inward prayer.

Here are some practical tips for how to cultivate this inward prayer and communion with God:

1. Meditate on the Word of God

In Joshua 1:8, God told the children of Israel:

> *Keep this Book of the Law always on your lips; meditate on it day and night, so that you may be careful to do everything written in it. Then you will be prosperous and successful.*

Inwardly meditating on Scripture and talking about Scripture with God is one simple way to build that inner dialogue with Him. God loves to talk to us about His Word and to hear our thoughts and questions about what it says.

2. Meditate on a Song

The psalmists wrote worship songs, but even when they weren't singing them in the public assembly, they would sing those songs inwardly to the Lord. About this, the psalmist Asaph wrote, "*I call to remembrance my song in the night; I meditate within my heart, and my spirit makes diligent search*" (Ps. 77:6 NKJV). We too can sing worship songs to God in our hearts while we go about our day—no matter where we are or what we're doing. Sometimes God will highlight a particular song, and it's like every time we hear that song, we feel a heart connect. We feel alive. What's happening is a back-and-forth exchange with God in which we're cultivating our relationship through that inward life of prayer.

3. Sing Spiritual Songs

Spiritual songs are like worship songs, except they originate in our own hearts, often spontaneously. They're not songs we learn from others but songs the Holy Spirit stirs up within us. Ephesians 5:18–20 tells us:

> ...Be filled with the Spirit, speaking to one another in psalms and hymns and spiritual songs, singing and making melody in your heart to the Lord, giving thanks always for all things to God the Father in the name of our Lord Jesus Christ.

Likewise, in Colossians 3:15–17, it says:

> Let the word of Christ dwell in you richly in all wisdom, teaching and admonishing one another in psalms and hymns and spiritual songs, singing with grace in your hearts to the Lord.

Spiritual songs well up within us as we meditate on God's Word and character. A song can easily get stuck in our heads, repeating over and over in our minds even when we're not consciously thinking about it. This can be annoying, depending on the song, but when it's a spiritual song about God, it is a glorious way to practice inward communion with Him. These songs that play though our heads all day go up as incense before the throne of grace. God hears and delights in that worship from our hearts.

4. Pray as Needs Arise

Sometimes we think we need to wait to pray about important matters until we're in our prayer closet and alone. It is much more effective for us to pray for issues that concern us as they arise. When we hear about a tragedy, we talk to God about it immediately. When we see a car accident, we pray as we drive by. When we don't know what to do in a certain situation, we ask God for help right away. We don't need to be in a special place for our prayers to have more impact.

Instead, our inward prayers that spring up from the secret place of our hearts are just as powerful as the prayers we pray in our prayer closets or in corporate gatherings. In fact, the prayers of our hearts are Revelation 5:8 prayers. They go up before the throne of God, causing our daily lives to carry the fragrance of God. When we are continually praying, we are continually accessing the presence of God, and as a result, we experience the reward of His abiding presence with us, day in and day out. That's what Brother Lawrence did. He practiced the presence of God in his daily life—whether he was washing the dishes or attending church services, he maintained continual communion with God.

5. Talk to Him about Everything

The Bible tells us, *"In all your ways acknowledge Him and He will direct your path"* (Prov. 3:6 NKJV). When we talk to God about everything, He will be with us and guide us. When we leave our prayer closet, we don't leave Jesus in the closet. He comes with us. As He promised, *"I will dwell in them and walk among them. I will be their God, and they shall be My people"* (2 Cor. 6:16). This means we can talk to God like we talk to our closest friends. God loves it when we include Him in our daily lives and talk to Him about even the seemingly mundane and boring details, because He wants to enter every detail of our lives with His goodness and His perspective. If we relegate Him to only the "spiritual" parts of our lives, we will miss out on so much.

I like to include God in every part of my life. I like shoes, so I talk to God about my shoes. I ask Him if He likes them. When I get into my car, I say, "Lord, where did I put my cell phone? Lord, what do You think about this outfit?" When I go to the health food store, I ask Him, "Lord, what do You think about this place?" I ask Him to help me see with His eyes and His heart, to see people the way He does. I ask Him, "What is Your will for my life today? Who do You want me to minister to?" This is what it can look like to cultivate the inward life of prayer. In every moment, my heart is pointed toward Him and inviting His involvement—in the big things and in the small.

This way of talking to God may seem crazy or irreverent to some people, but it's how I cultivate my inward life—by inviting Him into every part of it. Since I know Jesus is with me all the time, I act like He's there even though I can't see Him—which He is. And that means talking to Him about everything, just like I would with a friend who spent the day with me.

He is the kindest and most enjoyable friend we can find. And He never gets tired of going around with us, being with us in whatever we're doing. He never tires of helping me find my phone or giving me feedback on my outfit. He is that good. When we welcome Him in that completely, we will never be alone. He will make His presence so real to us, and as we commune with Him, our lives will be a fragrance of love to Him. I used to dislike being alone and often felt lonely, but now I really enjoy being alone, because when I'm alone I can focus on the inside of me, where Jesus lives.

When our bodies die, our spirits go to heaven to be with the Lord. Though we are already connected to Him while alive in our physical bodies, when our spirits go to Heaven, we finally get to meet Him face-to-face. When I stand before God, I want to already have an intimate knowledge of and relationship with Him. I don't want to arrive in Heaven and find myself standing before a perfect stranger. I want Him to already be my best friend. That is what the inward life of prayer and dialogue is all about.

CHAPTER 19

Returning to Love

It is easy, in the midst of busy lives, to lose our closeness with the Lord. We become distracted and, without even realizing it, we begin to drift. Jesus described this reality in the Parable of the Sower. The seed of His Word in our hearts can be choked if we allow the cares of life to captivate our attention and emotions:

> *Still others, like seed sown among thorns, hear the word; but the worries of this life, the deceitfulness of wealth and the desires for other things come in and choke the word, making it unfruitful* (Mark 4:18–19).

These things not only block our growth in the Word but also our growth in prayer. We get busy and become caught up in the things of this life instead of focusing on our relationship with Jesus. Though He has been so good to us, we forsake Him through neglect or distraction with other things. Anything we place in importance before the Lord—any person, possession, idea, or vision—has become an idol in our lives. When we give our attention to idols instead of God, we become like the children of Israel, who forsook God in exchange for worthless idols:

> *I remember the devotion of your youth, how as a bride you loved me and followed me through the wilderness.... But my people have exchanged their glorious God for worthless idols.... My people have committed two sins: They have forsaken me, the spring of living water, and have dug their own cisterns, broken cisterns that cannot hold water* (Jeremiah 2:2, 11, 13).

In this passage, God is crying out for His beloved to return to Him, for His people to return to their first love for Him. Jesus echoed this heart cry in His words to His followers in the first century church of Ephesus:

> *I know your deeds, your hard work and your perseverance. I know that you cannot tolerate wicked people, that you have tested those who claim to be apostles but are not, and have found them false. You have persevered and have endured hardships for my name, and have not grown weary. Yet I hold this against you: You have forsaken the love you had at first* (Revelation 2:2–4).

They had allowed the good and praiseworthy aspects of their church life and ministry to overshadow their actual love relationship with God. And while all of their hard work and perseverance for God's Kingdom was valuable, it was not as valuable as maintaining their passion for God. The first and most important thing is always our relationship with Him. If we neglect that, and instead try to earn His approval through obedience and diligence, we have forgotten what this faith is all about.

As we have talked about throughout this book, God longs for a deep and intimate love relationship with each one of us. We see this clearly in the story of the sisters Martha and Mary:

> As Jesus and his disciples were on their way, he came to a village where a woman named Martha opened her home to him. She had a sister called Mary, who sat at the Lord's feet listening to what he said. But Martha was distracted by all the preparations that had to be made. She came to him and asked, "Lord, don't you care that my sister has left me to do the work by myself? Tell her to help me!" "Martha, Martha," the Lord answered, "you are worried and upset about many things, but few things are needed—or indeed only one. Mary has chosen what is better, and it will not be taken away from her" (Luke 10:38–42).

Martha, like so many of us—in our responsibilities as women, wives, and moms—was distracted by all she had to do and missed the significance of who she had a chance to be with. God wants us to seek Him first and to know Him first, above all other people and responsibilities—just like Mary did. This doesn't mean meeting the needs of our families is unimportant. God wants us to take care of our responsibilities, but He wants us to do it from a place of communion with Him. He wants our love with Him to be our first priority.

Often, young girls walk very closely with God as children, but as they grow, they lose sight of God and His love. Without realizing it, they gradually drift from Him. As they grow older, they lose the innocent faith of childhood through the effect of peer pressure, boyfriends, and school work. In their teens, girls experience a great deal of pressure as they go through puberty and try to figure out their identity. It is an intense season, and in the midst of it, many young women walk away from God or lose the depth of intimacy they once had with Him. As they grow into womanhood and all the responsibilities involved, this distance is only reinforced.

But God does not give up on them, even when they walk away from Him. Instead, He tries to woo them back to Him and the innocence and depth of relationship they had with Him when they were young. We see God's intention in this matter so clearly in Hosea's prophecy:

> *"Therefore I am now going to allure her; I will lead her into the wilderness and speak tenderly to her....She will respond as in the days of her youth....In that day," declares the Lord, "you will call me 'my husband'; you will no longer call me 'my master.'...I will betroth you to me forever; I will betroth you in righteousness and justice, in love and compassion. I will betroth you in faithfulness, and you will acknowledge the Lord"* (Hosea 2:14–16, 19–20).

Like the prodigal son (see Luke 15:11–32), when we wander from God's embrace, He promises to allure us back to Himself by speaking tenderly to us—by showing us His beauty, grace, and love. He promises to welcome us back with open arms and to restore the passion we had for Him in the days of our youth. When we wander from God, He is not worried, because He knows how to reach our hearts. We are precious to Him, and what He began in our childhoods He will bring to fullness in us in adulthood. As He does, He will bring us into a fuller understanding of His love, and we will realize we are invited to call Him Husband (not Master), to rest in His love instead of working for His approval. This accurate picture of who God really is to us and His deep passion for us is designed to captivate our hearts for the rest of our lives.

When we find ourselves becoming distracted, the solution is simple. We return to His love. We turn ourselves around and head back toward His embrace. When I find myself distant from God, my solution is to renew my vows with Him, like I mentioned briefly in Chapter 12. The first time I did this, I bought a special ring and had a renewal ceremony in my prayer room—just like when a couple renews their marriage vows. As part of the ceremony, I took communion and read certain Scriptures that declare my commitment to and love for God as my husband. I even played the song "Dance with Me" and envisioned myself dancing with my Lord. As we dance, I say "I do" again. I tell Him He is my first and greatest love, and I rest in His loving embrace. Once again, I am in my place of greatest peace and joy and freedom. I am in the arms of passion Himself, and He makes me come alive.

Who would not want to return to a love like that?

Conclusion

We are daughters of a good God! What an incredible revelation. God our Father loves us with an everlasting and unconditional love. It cannot be shaken, and it does not need to be earned. It simply is. With His great arms of love, God waits for each one of us. He longs to envelope us in His love, to wash away the pain and the scars from imperfect lovers, and to fill us with His vision of ourselves. He is eager to teach us about the freedom we will find in seeing ourselves the way He does. If we will believe what He says, that simple belief will change our lives completely. We will realize who He is and who we are in Him, and we will stop listening to lies. We will be transformed by the power of His love.

Yet this transformation is only the beginning—an invitation into the best life we could ever know. It is like the wedding day, when a woman takes her new husband's name as her own. Her identity has changed with the advent of her marriage. Now she must work with her husband to cultivate their love into a deep and strong intimacy that cannot be shaken. So too, the revelation of our new identity as royalty, as beloved daughters of the King, is the beginning of a lifelong adventure into the heart of God. We bear His name, and He lives in our hearts. Every day, He invites us to walk with Him, to cultivate an intimate friendship with Him.

What about you? Will you say yes?

Endnotes

1. Saint Augustine, "Let Us Sing to the Lord a Song of Love," from Sermo 34.1–3, 5–6; CCL 41, 424–426.

2. Definitions of these words are taken from Kenneth Wuest, *Wuest's Word Studies in the Greek New Testament*, Vol. 3 (Grand Rapids, MI: Wm. B. Eerdmans Publishing Co,. 1975), 111–113.

3. *Blue Letter Bible*, John 21:15–17.

4. For further reading on this subject, see E.W. Kenyon, *The Bible in the Light of Our Redemption* (Kenyons Gospel Publishing Society, 2011).

5. *The Dake Annotated Reference Bible* (Dake Bible Sales, 1996).

6. Brian and Jenn Johnson, "Love Came Down," *Love Came Down* (Bethel Music, 2010), track 1.

7. T.D. Jakes, "You Don't Have to Believe in My Dream," audio CD teaching. Also, I highly recommend T.D. Jakes' book, *Woman Thou Art Loosed!* (Shippensburg, PA: Destiny Image, 1993).

8. "Child Abuse Facts," *Safe Horizon*, http://www.safehorizon.org/index/what-we-do-2/child-abuse--incest-55/child-abuse-statistics--facts-304.html.

9. "The Names of God in the Old Testament," *Blue Letter Bible*, http://www.blueletterbible.org/study/misc/name_god.cfm; See also Joyce Meyer's CD teaching series, "Knowing God Intimately by Understanding His Name."

10. *Blue Letter Bible*, John 1:18, s.v. "horao" (G3708); "exegeomai" (G1834).

11. US Bureau of the Census, "Who's minding the kids?" (1994).

12. *Blue Letter Bible*, s.v. "Charitoo" (G5487).

13. For more information on biblical submission, I recommend these books: *Why Not Women?* (Loren Cunningham and David Joel Hamilton, Seattle, WA: 2000) and *Powerful and Free* (Danny Silk, Redding, CA: 2012).

14. To women who are in abusive relationships, I recommend these books: *Healing the Scars of Emotional Abuse* (Gregory L. Jantz, with Ann McMurray, MI: 1995) and *No Visible Wounds* (Mary Susan Miller, New York: 1995).

15. Paul Wilbur, "Show Me Your Face," *Lion of Judah* (Hosanna!/Epic, 2002), track 9.

16. Andrew Murray, quoted in Mark Water, *Encyclopedia of Prayer and Praise* (UK: 2004), 1164.

17. For more on this, see my book *Encounter God Through the Habit of Prayer* (2011).

18. Leonard Ravenhill, quoted in Mark Water, *Encyclopedia of Prayer and Praise*., 1170.

19. An excellent book on this topic is the classic by Andrew Murray, *The Inner Chamber* (Fort Washington, PA: Christian Literature Crusade, 1981).

About Margie Fleurant

Author, founder, and president of The River Ministries, Margie Fleurant speaks in the prophetic voice, challenging and building up the body of Christ through keen biblical insights. Margie's messages and books inspire and ignite a deeper passion for the Lord. In them people discover how to study and meditate on Scripture in order to uncover a more vibrant faith and intimate prayer time with the Lord. All of her teachings are grounded on the timeless principles of the Word of God. She often teaches on how to hear and understand the heart of the Father and how to realize His desire to see His people fulfill their ordained purposes here on earth.

Prayer is the cornerstone of The River Ministries, and Margie has shared its importance with congregations throughout the United States and overseas. Her series of books on prayer— *Marked for Intercession*, *Prayer for the Ministry Gifts*, and *Encounter God Through the Habit of Prayer*—give clear evidence that Margie is a woman who is uncompromisingly devoted to preaching the gospel message with authority and simplicity. The revelations she shares bring power and victory to people of faith no matter how long they have been on their spiritual journey. Traveling extensively as a keynote speaker, Margie uses the prophetic gifts the Lord has given her to creatively share messages with youth and adults in relevant ways. She has been the main speaker at many churches, Women's Conferences, Youth Conferences, and Weekend Prayer Seminars throughout the United States. Margie recently traveled to Guatemala as one of the guest speakers at the Living Water Bible Teaching Institute in May of 2013.

Margie graduated from Rhema Bible Training Center in 1977 and is an ordained minister through Covenant Ministries International. She is also an ordained member of Faith Covenant Ministries. Margie and her husband, John, currently reside in New Jersey and have three grown children.

OTHER TITLES BY
Margie Fleurant

Marked for Intercession

In this book, Margie, writes from a place of authority,  knowing and walking in her true calling in Christ. She is a seasoned intercessor that desires to share the Father's heart with her readers. To intercede is to "stand in the gap for those in need," and when done correctly, it is a powerful means of prayer. Margie delves into the little-known ministry of intercession; how this ministry relates to Jesus, and why it is relevant to believers today.

It is the mission of this book is to reveal to the believer the greatest act of love, which is found in the power of persistent prayer on behalf of their families, neighbors, friends, cities and nations. Readers will gain biblical insight into how to pray effectively.

Prayer for the Ministry Gifts

A book written specifically for ministry leaders.  Church leaders need the appropriate prayer support from faithful congregants. In this book, gain insight into how the call of God effects the heart of a minister. Discover how this call motivates the leader as you prayerfully support them in fulfilling their destiny, affecting the church body as a whole.

Encounter God Through the Habit of Prayer

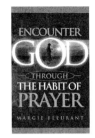

Many people possess a certain reverence for God, yet they view Him as a distant personality who's disinterested in the daily activities of their lives. Many are going through life unfulfilled, their spiritual hunger unsatisfied. They haven't learned the truth that God desires to walk with them in real, intimate fellowship. Learn how to experience a matchless companionship with the Lord that is anchored in prayer and vital to the human experience.

En Encontrar a Dios Mediante el Hábito de la Oración

Mucha gente posee una cierta reverencia hacia Dios, pero solamente lo ven como un personaje distante a quien no le interesan las actividades diarias de nuestras vidas. Muchos pasan por la vida vacíos, y con un hambre espiritual insatisfecha. No han descubierto la verdad de que Dios desea caminar con ellos en una comunión intima y real. Todavía no han experimentado su compañía incomparable la cual es tan vital para la vida humana.

The Art of Intercession Study Guide

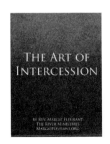

This is a detailed study guide for people who want to dive into God's Word and study the topic of prayer. In this booklet, readers will learn about the different kinds of prayer, the foundations needed for prayer and the power being an intercessor allows you to tap into as you pray to The Lord.

A Love Like That

To purchase additional teaching materials
or to schedule a speaking engagement,
please contact Margie at:
www.MargieFleurant.org